Contemporary Teddy Bear Price Guide

Artists to Manufacturers

by Terry & Doris Michaud

Published by 

Hobby House Press, Inc.
Cumberland, Maryland 21502

DEDICATION

This book is dedicated to the memory of the late James Martin, and to Winifred Martin, Doris's mother and late father. Doris learned her sewing and design skills from her father, who had tailoring experience, and she inherited her deep sense of caring and sharing from her mother.

ACKNOWLEDGMENTS

The authors wish to thank the many people whose contributions made this book possible. Our thanks to Gary and Mary Ruddell and their excellent staff at Hobby House Press, Inc.; to Dottie Ayers, Donna Harrison West, and Paul and Rosemary Volpp for sharing some of their materials and photos from their wonderful book **Teddy Bear Artists Annual**; to Thomas Mocny for his outstanding cover photography; to Ken Hornak, Jr. of Starfire Software for his assistance in developing the computer programs used in compiling the price information; to our daughter Mary Baese and her husband Dennis for processing the computer data; to our daughter Pat Messinger and her husband Mike for managing to keep everything flowing in the right direction; and to the host of artists, manufacturers and their representatives for supplying the raw data needed to put this whole thing together.

Other people have been cited in various sections for specific contributions, but it would be impossible to list everyone who aided in the project. Our gratitude goes to anyone we may have neglected to mention. Most of all, we want to thank the arctophiles who support the work being done by artists and designers around the world.

Additional copies of this book may be purchased at $16.95
from
HOBBY HOUSE PRESS, INC.
900 Frederick Street
Cumberland, Maryland 21502
or from your favorite bookstore or dealer.
Please add $4.75 per copy for postage.

Printed in the United States of America

ISBN: 0-87588-398-2

FOREWORD
THE FUTURE OF TEDDY BEAR COLLECTING

Our avocation (or vocation for some) has experienced phenomenal growth over the past few years, with collector enthusiasm reaching new heights with each passing month. We are frequently asked if the hobby has peaked, and it is our opinion that it will continue to grow as new collectors come in to our ranks. It is inevitable we will lose some artists and bear makers to burnout, and some collectors will change the course of their collecting. But with new collectors joining our ranks every day, and with collectors discovering a hidden talent for designing and making bears, the future of our hobby is indeed secure.

As stated, this is our opinion. To confirm this outlook, we went to a number of experts from various disciplines within our field. Each was asked the same questions; "How do you see the future of teddy bear collecting?" This is what we learned.

From Bruce S. Raiffe of Gund, Inc.: "Gund is in a unique position within the bear world. As a company that has been in existence since 1898, we have found that many of our bears, which were not originally designed as collectibles, have become just that by virtue of their longevity.

We have witnessed the rise of bear collecting, with antique teddy bears garnering increasing prices at auction houses. Most recently, the proliferation of American bear artists has contributed to the wealth of limited production bears that collectors seek.

Through the wide distribution of Gund products, arctophiles have greater access to the limited edition collectors bears that are available through Gund. Canterbury Bears, Bialosky Bears and the Gund Signature Collection have loyal followings that are growing in numbers. Even Winnie-the-Pooh collectors find they have a number of Gund Poohs in their collection.

Because of the personal relationship people have with their childhood bears, the future of teddy bear collecting is secure. Collectors extend that personal relationship into adulthood, with every new acquisition becoming an instant member of the family.

Bear collecting is also comparable to traditional collecting. Bear collectors also look for quality, longevity and value.

Whatever the reason for getting started, once someone finds the right bear to love, they become a collector for life."

BRUCE S. RAIFFE
Executive Vice President
Gund, Inc.
Edison, New Jersey

From Beth Savino, sponsor of the highly regarded The Toy Store Tribute To Teddies: "It is really amazing to me that collector and artist bears have been a part of "Tribute to Teddies," our show in Toledo for 11 years. At first, they joined the dolls on a trial basis and were not even mentioned by name in our advertising. Our Steiff collector's business had just begun with the 1980 introduction of "Papa" bear, and we discovered there were people out there who loved teddy bears and wanted a nostalgic, quality bear.

My personal interest was piqued by Peggy and Alan Bialosky's first book. The Steiff stimulus was given a jump start with Jean Wilson and Shirley Conway's one hundred year tribute book.

About this same time, we were fortunate to buy, on the recommendation of the Bialoskys, our first artists bears from Carrousel and the Michauds. This fortunate turn of events led to the Bialoskys and the Michauds making personal appearances at our show. People flocked to see them. Our very first Limited Edition *Jester* a lovely black fellow, was created for us by the Michauds. I was worried, because although I loved him, he was not a Steiff. I wish I had a few hundred of them to sell today!

Over the years, we have done some wonderful projects with Steiff, Merrythought, Hermann and Gund. Artists such as Linda Spiegel Lohr, Jenny and Dick Krantz, Monty and Joe Sours, Linda Henry, Bonnie Hotchkin, Remi Kramer, John and Maude Blackburn, Sue Foskey, and Joyce Haughey have done wonderful pieces for us. *Buckeye Billy* by the Michauds sold out in under two hours at our 1991 show!

I have seen tremendous growth on the part of the artist as well as the collector. Today's artists, by the hundreds, are creating many wonderful, imaginative works of art. The collector has become much more discriminating.

Artist bears have challenged the makers of collector bears to be more exacting in their standards of quality and imagination."

BETH SAVINO
The Toy Store
Toledo, Ohio

From well-known bear artists Sue and Randall Foskey: "We see the future of the artist bears as growing larger and more complex. There are so many artists with so many ideas. It appears that artist bears have captured a large part of the market. As more people are becoming knowledgeable of the artists and their work, their bears are becoming more in demand. We also see the manufacturers starting to recognize the artist as well. Many artists are being commissioned by large manufacturers to design for them or have their designs reproduced by them. This is good recognition for the artist, increasing the value of their own artist-produced lines.

We see the bear business running neck to neck with the doll business in every aspect; antiques, modern artist and collectibles."

SUE AND RANDALL FOSKEY
Nostalgic Bear Company
Ocean View, Delaware

Donna Harrison West, sponsor of the popular Baltimore Convention and Show: "In my opinion the really good bear artists who do quality workmanship with creative designing will become the desired future artists by the collectors. It is just the same with the fine art market. When you buy a contemporary painting, you gamble that investment wise, others will think the same and continue to promote the particular artist, thus making their work become more valuable.

Antique bears needed to level out. Prices got crazy for awhile. They will always be good investments if the collector buys condition and quality because there are just so many to choose from. Supply and demand will thus keep the prices steady on your good antiques in any field. New collectors are constantly entering the hobby, wanting top-quality antique bears and willing to pay any price for them.

I see a good future for the collectible bear market, with more and more enthusiastic people participating in the fun of teddy bear collecting."

DONNA HARRISON WEST
Baltimore, Maryland

From Robert Raikes, creator and designer of Raikes Bears: "As we race along in our modern world, in some of us there is a bittersweet longing for those gentle moments of our past. The time of innocents, the times with loved ones now departed, old friends remembered, the hug of a grandparent, and falling asleep with one's teddy bear.

For today's collector, the teddy bear is a wonderful bridge to that nostalgic past. For today's artist, the teddy bear is a means of expression, a hint giver of the inner person's values and feelings.

This art form continues to expand and grow. New talented people are constantly entering the arena. Those of us who have been working at our art for years continue to build on a foundation of experience and relationships. The message conveyed by the teddy bear artist is slowly expanding outside the traditional circle of teddy bear collectors, as new people find the magic of our furry friends."

ROBERT RAIKES

From Linda Farley, operator of Bears 'N Wares, one of the country's leading teddy bear specialty shops: "The artist bear, whether entirely made by the artist or designed by the artist, has definitely found its place high on the list among collectors. The true artist is one who displays a sense of "art" in his/her work, and I strongly believe the future will be very promising for those who possess a talent for both unique, artistic designs, bears filled with personality, reproduction of some of the great designs of yesteryear, together with superior quality and appropriate pricing.

Nationally advertised work should, of course, be longer remembered. Today's collector is more discriminating than ever; and, even though investment value is an important issue most collectors continue to make their purchases based on the appeal of the bear.

My final opinion is that the artist market is strong, will continue to gain strength and that quality and design will be of the utmost importance in the future. My personal advice has always been to invest in the love and enjoyment of collecting, and you will never have made a wrong purchase."

LINDA FARLEY
Bears 'N Wears
New Cumberland, Pennsylvania

From ABC Unlimited Productions, sponsors of teddy bear shows from coast to coast: "For the past decade the teddy bear market — artist made bears as well as manufactured collectibles — has enjoyed a steady growth and respectability. However, over the past year and a half we have been witnessing certain changes that indicate a need to reevaluate this industry's marketing philosophy. Teddy bear collectors are becoming more discerning about quality, materials, and price. The more sophisticated the collector, the more selective they become, buying fewer better quality or more expensive bears. Hence, there is a necessity to develop a larger collector base by both introducing more people to the wonderful world of teddy bears and creating quality collectible bears priced to attract a wider range of collectors.

In order to accomplish this, it is essential for the artists as well as the manufacturers, to take a good look at the market. For the more established artists to continue their success, they need to keep in mind that most new collectors wade into the waters, not dive in. For those artists who are newcomers, they need to recognize that they have to earn their stripes and keep their product at a price point commensurate with their stature in the industry.

In short, this industry while still in a growth pattern needs to consider economic swings and emotional environment unique to this sector of the retail market and react quickly to these changes in order to continue its viability."

AMBER BEELER
CONNIE BROUILLETTE
ABC Unlimited Productions
Floosmoor, Illinois

From Ron Block and his lovely wife Elke, who supply a vast number of teddy bear artists with quality mohair and other supplies under the trade name Edinburgh Imports, Inc.: "The first teddy bear artists will remain anonymous, and will exist only as the creative spirits behind early manufactured bears which began our wonderful world. It was not until some 80 years later, when the bearmakers who searched flea markets, attics and Salvation Army stores for the wonderful old fabrics, began to find high-quality mohair and alpaca available. These supplies, available in quantity in the early 1980s, allowed artists the creative ability to make bears that matched, or surpassed the high-quality perception of manufactured collector bears in the eyes of the collector. The individualistic art form of bearmaking began to unfold.

The true beginnings of artist bear acceptance and growth is not quite ten years old as I write this. As with most art forms in their infancy, the growth and success are far from understood, and just beginning to be achieved.

I am confident that tomorrow will have within its framework a formal recognition of this soft-sculpture art form. We began as a small part of the fourth largest collectible in the world — teddy bears, and our future has just begun."

RON BLOCK
Edinburgh Imports Inc.
Calabasas, California

INTRODUCTION

One of the most often asked questions of artists and shop owners is this; "Will today's artist and collector bears appreciate in value?" We can say with every confidence, the answer is yes. If you think about it, every antique sold today (teddy bear or otherwise) was new at one time. Now as to accurately predicting how soon a contemporary bear will increase in value, or how much, that is a bit more difficult to deal with. We hope this price guide will help to do just that. Please note, it is not our intention to set secondary market prices. We have based our estimate of current market values on a wide variety of factors, many of the same factors that help to predict the rise in price of other collectibles, including dolls.

How can a novice collector assure that they are building a collection that will increase in value? There are a number of factors to consider, but the number one factor to assure this is knowledge. Talk to advanced collectors and you will find that for the most part, they are very knowledgeable about the particular brands of collector bears they are building on, as well as the artist/artists they favor. The best way to protect your investment is to learn everything you can about the subject. How do you do that? One of the best ways is to join a teddy bear club, particularly a club that specializes in the make or type of bear you want to collect. Many of these clubs supply their members with a newsletter or magazine containing articles that detail any new developments with a particular bear, or biographies of other collectors and lessons they have gained through past show experiences. One of the big pluses in being associated with this field is that arctophiles tend to be very open and sharing with their knowledge.

Another major source of information are shows and conventions, both on the regional and national level. We have been collecting for around 20 years, and yet continue to learn every time we attend a convention. It can be somewhat expensive to attend a convention, particularly if you have to travel some distance, but it is worth the expense if the convention serves as a learning experience to make you a better collector.

Specialty shops and those who sell collector and artist bears also provide a wealth of information. They have made it their business to know about the product they are selling, and since many of these merchants are also collectors, they too are very sharing with information. It has become common practice for many shops to sponsor a special appearance by one or more artists and/or collector bear company representatives for one or more days during a shop event. These are always well worth your time to attend, even if your budget does not allow for a purchase at that particular time. It will give you an opportunity to talk directly with the artist or representative that you might not otherwise have the chance to meet.

Do not overlook the most obvious learning opportunity; that is to talk to other collectors. Back in the late 1970s when this current craze was little known, Doris and I were set up at a fairgrounds antique show in Ohio. We were both wearing hand-painted T-shirts that showed a teddy bear holding a sign that read "Wanted — old teddy bears." A delightful couple approached us, and seeing the sign, struck up a conversation that blossomed into a very close friendship. That couple was Peggy and Alan Bialosky! Next time you find yourself in the presence of another collector (at a shop or a show) introduce yourself. Ask how long they have been collecting, what bears they favor, and if they belong to a club.

While on the subject of clubs, I would be remiss if I did not mention my favorite club, "Good Bears of the World." This nonprofit club devotes their time and energy to supplying teddy bears to children in hospitals, to police agencies who use them in traumatic situations involving children, and to the elderly in nursing homes. I can think of no better way of spreading the love that comes from teddy bears than to participate in this grand organization (see "Information Please" section). If you are geographically situated where a chapter does not exist, you can participate by mail. They also have a quarterly magazine for members that always contains helpful information on collecting.

Yet another source for information on collecting are books and magazines. Publications devoted to the hobby such as *Teddy Bear and friends®* magazine provide a wealth of information for both the new and advanced collector. In addition to articles by knowledgeable writers, you will find patterns and instructions to make your own bear. Books are also an important learning tool, and there are books covering just about every phase of this hobby. Many of the shops that specialize in teddy bears also offer the newest books on the subject. These books can also be found at shows, and through magazines dealing with the subject.

Finally, a word on what to look for, what to buy, etc. It has always been our recommendation that a collector should first analyze their long term goals. If they simply love bears, and do not have a concern about their manufacturing process or material, then by all means, buy the least expensive bears (those that are mass produced) and enjoy your collection. If your goal is to build a collection that will perhaps some day mature in value, then buy the very best quality you can afford. Pay particular attention to the material the bear is made of. If it is mohair, alpaca or some other quality natural fibre, its worth will increase much more than one produced in acrylic or a man-made fabric. Examine the bear carefully. Are the seams well stitched, even and brushed out to make them not quite so noticeable? Are the joints nice and tight? Are the eyes glass or plastic? Is the bear well-designed? Another important factor is the maker. Does this artist or manufacturer have a good track record for producing quality work? This is not to say that new artists are not to be considered, because if you are fortunate enough to choose a bear by an upcoming artist that in years coming will be highly sought after, then your collection will be enriched by having one of this artist's earlier works.

Price also has to be a consideration when choosing a bear. The value of the bear will undoubtedly vary with each collector, but you should be able to compare the bear you want to buy with others of equal quality by an artist or maker with equal reputation. The artist or manufacturer's reputation and experience, and the number of bears being marketed, are just a few of the factors used to determine a fair market price. The collector is the most important determining factor, for if the bear is overpriced and does not sell, it sends a message to the maker. If, however, you feel it is overpriced, and shortly thereafter a collector buys it, then maybe your expectations are not realistic.

This price guide took the unusual approach to determining current market values by creating a computer program, based on over fifteen factors to arrive at the final price. Each and every artist/producer was treated equally. The actual program is proprietary, but some of the factors included: age of the bear, original price, material of construction, number of pieces produced, etc. Experience and reputation were also considered. Before proceeding, we want to clarify some definitions. To say there is disagreement on what or who an artist bear maker is, would be an understatement. Some feel strongly that to be called an artist bear, it has to have been not only designed, but completely made in its entirety by the artist. Some collectors have made it known that they consider it an artist bear if it was designed by and at least finished by the artist, even though others may have been involved in some of the initial cutting and sewing, stuffing, etc. *The Merriam Webster Dictionary* proclaims art as a skill acquired by experience or study; the use of skill and imagination in the production of things of beauty. It further states that an artist is one who practices an art, one who creates objects of beauty. Personally, we do not have any major feelings one way or the other, for I think our work will be judged many years from now by people who are not emotionally involved.

For the purposes of this price guide, we define the **artist bear** as one that has been made entirely or partially by the artist, and the **collector bear** as one that has been designed by one person, but produced or made by one or more persons without assistance by the artist/designer.

As stated earlier, it is not our intention to set prices on the secondary market. Only time and actual sales will determine this value. Prices will also vary by region, just as they do with antique teddy bears. This guide simply weighs a variety of factors to predict what the current "worth" of a given bear is. You may find the bear to be sold at a higher or lower price.

This guide is by no means all inclusive. Two major mailings were done to reach artists and manufacturers, and unfortunately a number of producers were missed. We therefore apologize to anyone who was not included, as it was not our intention to exclude anyone. Where previous secondary market knowledge was available, it has been used and acknowledged. All other current market values have been determined by our computer program.

SECTION ONE

ARTIST TEDDY BEARS

This section contains a listing of teddy bears produced entirely or in part by the designer/artist bear maker.

Please note that in the case of open edition bears, or bears still available from the artist or their designated agent, the current value listed applies only to the bears produced during the year of introduction and only to those in mint condition with all original boxes, certificates and tags. Teddy bears of the same issue produced in subsequent years, or in condition less than original, would reflect a current value of a lower amount.

Little Bear Peep
8in (20cm) fully-jointed bear made with acrylic cream fur. Pink dress with flower peplins and matching bonnet and pantaloons.
INTRODUCED: 1987
PRODUCTION: 150
ORIGINAL PRICE: $100.00
CURRENT VALUE: $225.00

ADAMS, JOANNE
P.O. Box 68-1027
Park City, Utah 84068
TRADE NAME: Storybook Bears
Joanne received a small doll at age seven and spent many happy hours making dresses, accessories, and many costumes for it. As a young adult, she found herself designing and producing clothes, toys, costumes and accessories for children. After moving from California to Utah with her husband and four children, she was inspired by a friend to make teddy bears, and so the cycle of designing and producing clothes and costumes continues!
Photograph by Patrick McDowell.

ALBERSTADT, BARBARA

73 Melissa Road
Kingston, New York 12401

TRADE NAME: Catskill Honey Bears

Barbara and her husband live in the beautiful Catskills. With a strong background in art and sewing, Barbara purchased a bear making kit in 1984, and although she was not very pleased with the results, it was enough to get her started. When her daughter married, her room became the "bear factory," and Barbara was off on a new adventure. The love of creating keeps Barbara striving for that perfect bear. Since her bear making time is limited, she does small editions of each design, with more ideas than time to spend making them.

Molassis
17in (43cm) fully-jointed bear with acrylic red-brown fur.
INTRODUCED: 1988
PRODUCTION: Limited Edition 65
ORIGINAL PRICE: $65.00
CURRENT VALUE: $125.00

Raspbeary Bear
10in (25cm) fully-jointed bear made of mohair fabric.
INTRODUCED: 1988
PRODUCTION: Open Edition
ORIGINAL PRICE: $50.00
CURRENT VALUE: $90.00

Raspbeary Bear
12in (31cm)
ORIGINAL PRICE: $60.00
CURRENT VALUE: $100.00

ALLEN, DARLENE

4756A East Ekahi Way
Ewa Beach, Hawaii 96706

TRADE NAME: Raspbeary Bears

Although originally from Cincinnati, Ohio, Darlene currently resides in Hawaii with her Navy husband and two children. She has a business degree from the University of Cincinnati and has been a bear artist since the early 1980s. *Photographs by Keith Allen.*

ALLEN, DURAE

1037 Beechfield Avenue
Baltimore, Maryland 21229

TRADE NAME: Lil' Honeys by Durae

The first Lil' Honey Bear came to life in October 1985. Since then Durae has combined her designing ability and sewing talent to create a full-time teddy bear business. Working eight hours a day, Durae strives for the highest standards to meet the demands of the most sophisticated collectors. Durae travels to shows and conventions throughout the United States. Although the birth of her daughter Brittany slowed her down some, Durae feels that she now motivates her to become more innovative. Her bears range in size from 1/2in (1cm) to 5ft (155cm) in size and vary from simple bears with no trimming to elaborately dressed pieces. Durae limits her editions so she can continue to produce new designs for collectors. *Photographs by Durae Allen.*

Daffiny and Unicorn Bear
Daffiny 6in (15cm), ***Unicorn*** 8in (20cm). ***Daffiny*** is a fully-jointed mohair bear wearing an aqua lace and peach eyelet party dress with satin ribbons and rosebuds. ***Unicorn*** is of alpaca fabric with mohair mane.
INTRODUCED: Fall 1988
PRODUCTION: Limited Edition 6 sets
ORIGINAL PRICE: $350.00 set
CURRENT VALUE: $825.00 set

Sabrina On Her Carrousel
9in (23cm) fully-jointed bent leg bear. Bear is of creamy mohair, wearing a mauve and green satin dress. She sits on a brown merino wool Carrousel Bear. Base and pole of oak.
INTRODUCED: February 1988
PRODUCTION: Limited Edition 100 sets
ORIGINAL PRICE: $350.00 set
CURRENT VALUE: $850.00 set

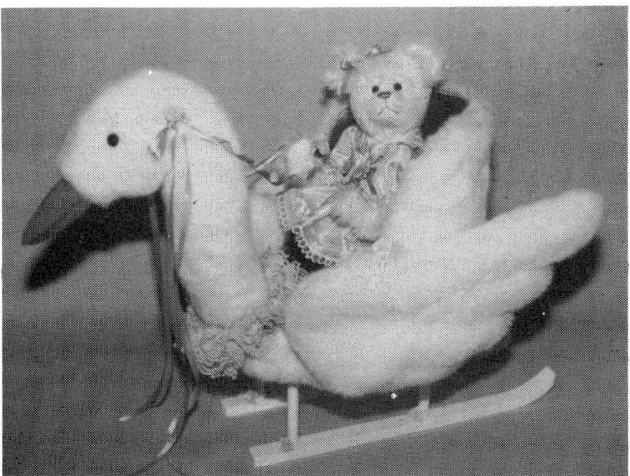

Tiffany and Her Swan Sleigh
Jointed white mohair bear 9in (23cm) in size, wearing a pastel blue moiree taffeta dress trimmed in pink ribbons and rosettes. Swan sleigh is made of synthetic European plush with pink satin interior.
INTRODUCED: December 1988
PRODUCTION: Limited Edition 75
ORIGINAL PRICE: $350.00
CURRENT VALUE: $825.00

Fiesty
7in (18cm) fully-jointed bear made of 40% mohair and 60% wool from an old coat.
INTRODUCED: 1986
PRODUCTION: Limited Edition 10
ORIGINAL PRICE: $45.00
CURRENT VALUE: $100.00

Wool Bears
6in (15cm). One of the earliest Lil' Honeys ever made, produced from old coats and identified with leatherette bear shaped tag with initials WB. Each was individually costumed.
INTRODUCED: January 1988
PRODUCTION: 77
ORIGINAL PRICE: $40.00
CURRENT VALUE: $75.00

Bittersweet Bears
8½in (22cm) jointed bears made from an old coat.
INTRODUCED: January 1986
ORIGINAL PRICE: $39.95 each
CURRENT VALUE: $100.00 each

ALTHERR, TERRI L.

RR #3, Box 206
Elwood, Indiana 46036

TRADE NAME: Panda Monium

Terri Altherr has been a panda collector for over 21 years, but it was not until 1984 that she purchased a kit and tried her hand at making a panda. It was never finished. In 1985 she attended a teddy convention and participated in a workshop, and this time she was inspired to continue. Although not happy with her early attempts at pattern making, Teri persisted, and today her bears are popular with collectors everywhere. Terri makes bears ranging in size from 2in to 36in (5cm to 91cm), using a variety of fabrics which include mohair, alpaca, synthetics, velvets, ultra suede, and even old coat fabrics. She keeps her editions small, preferring to do editions of five pieces, and needless to say, the panda is her favorite to do. Terri gets support from her family, with joints made by her husband Bill, and tags made by her daughter Amanda.

Panda
10½in (27cm). Jointed, made with mohair.
INTRODUCED: December 1988
ORIGINAL PRICE: $79.95
CURRENT VALUE: $175.00

Panda
8in (20cm). Jointed, made with mohair.
INTRODUCED: January 1988
ORIGINAL PRICE: $49.95
CURRENT VALUE: $100.00

Ping Ping Panda
12in (31cm) panda made with German synthetic and alpaca, jointed.
INTRODUCED: 1988
ORIGINAL PRICE: $99.95
CURRENT VALUE: $225.00

Bearon
36in (91cm) jointed bear, made with mohair.
INTRODUCED: November 1988
ORIGINAL PRICE: $200.00
CURRENT VALUE: $425.00

Panda
22in (56cm). Jointed, made with mohair
INTRODUCED: 1986
PRODUCTION: One-of-a-kind
ORIGINAL PRICE: $125.00
CURRENT VALUE: $225.00

BABB, DIANE
1126 Ivon Avenue
Endicott, New York 13760
TRADE NAME: J.D. Babb, Inc.
Diane studied at the Art Institute of Chicago. Her love of wildlife led to designing realistic soft sculpture animals and teddy bears. Moving to New York with her husband Jim and four children, she decided to use her talent to help with college expenses. Within a short time she was accepted into prestigious craft shows on the East coast. She was among the first artists recognized as designing modern day collectible bears. Her bears can be found in collections across America and as far away as Germany, Japan, Australia, Saudi Arabia and England.

Bride and Groom
Bride is 14in (36cm) tall, made in off-white dense mohair. ***Groom*** is 16in (41cm) tall in light, dense caramel mohair. Wearing fully-lined jacket, long pants, long sleeve shirt, cummerbund and bow tie.
INTRODUCED: 1988
PRODUCTION: Limited Edition 10 sets
ORIGINAL PRICE: $475.00 set
CURRENT VALUE: $1225.00 set

Edward
20in (51cm) bear jointed at arms and legs, made of synthetic long pile fur with short pile snout.
INTRODUCED: 1986
PRODUCTION: 25
ORIGINAL PRICE: $125.00
CURRENT VALUE: $375.00

Edmond
14in (36cm) bear jointed at arms and legs, made of synthetic long pile fur with short pile snout.
INTRODUCED: 1986
PRODUCTION: 50
ORIGINAL PRICE: $90.00
CURRENT VALUE: $275.00

Bruino
28in (71cm) tall, constructed of long pile synthetic fur with short pile snout. Paw pads and markings of Spanish suede, with markings padded and hand sewn. Safety locked nose and eyes, fully jointed.
INTRODUCED: 1982
PRODUCTION: 25
ORIGINAL PRICE: $95.00
CURRENT VALUE: $450.00

Babbaer
Made in a variety of colors of long pile synthetic furs, fully-jointed.
INTRODUCED: 1977
PRODUCTION: Approximately 300
ORIGINAL PRICE: $35.00
CURRENT VALUE: $300.00

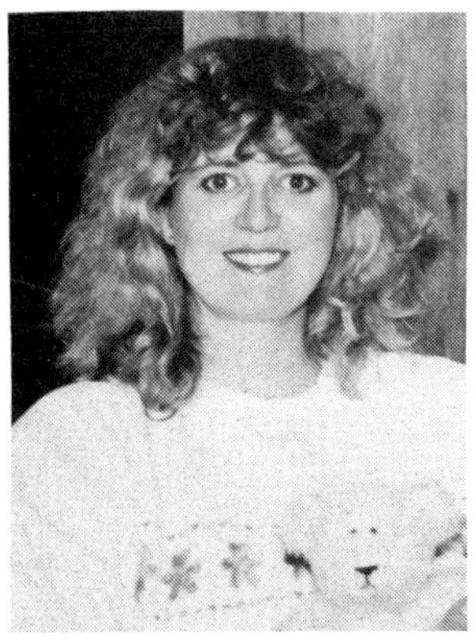

BAKER, SUSAN

387 S. Fourth Avenue
Middleport, Ohio 45760

TRADE NAME: The Ohio River Bear Company
Starting in the mid 1980s, Susan switched careers from photographer to teddy bear maker. She states she is still not quite sure how it happened, but she is glad it did. Susan is married, has four children, and lives in a big, old brick house in a small town in Ohio. *Photographs by Susan Baker.*

Robin
Jointed 10in (25cm) short mohair bear.
INTRODUCED: 1988
ORIGINAL PRICE: $45.00
CURRENT VALUE: $100.00

Dylan
Jointed 10in (25cm) bear in long mohair.
INTRODUCED: 1988
ORIGINAL PRICE: $50.00
CURRENT VALUE: $100.00

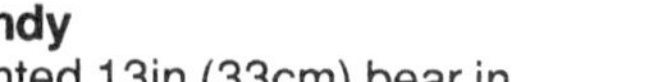

Candy
Jointed 13in (33cm) bear in acrylic fur.
INTRODUCED: 1988
PRODUCTION: Unlimited Production
ORIGINAL PRICE: $24.00
CURRENT VALUE: $50.00

Ned
Jointed 15in (38cm) bear in acrylic fur.
INTRODUCED: 1988
PRODUCTION: Unlimited Production
ORIGINAL PRICE: $30.00
CURRENT VALUE: $50.00

Uncle Edgar
12in (31cm) jointed bear in acrylic fur.
INTRODUCED: 1988
PRODUCTION: Unlimited Production
ORIGINAL PRICE: $25.00
CURRENT VALUE: $50.00

Mickey
5in (13cm) jointed bear in acrylic fur.
INTRODUCED: 1988
PRODUCTION: Unlimited Production
ORIGINAL PRICE: $10.00
CURRENT VALUE: $25.00

BALDO, MARY FRAN

89 West Bonanza Place
Battlement Mesa, Colorado 81636
TRADE NAME: M.F.B. Enterprises

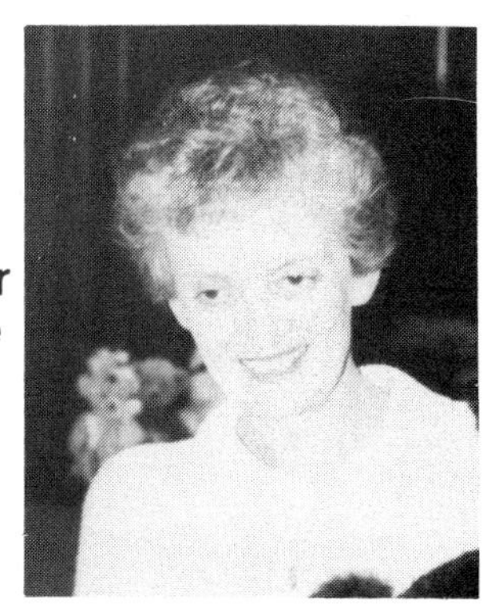

Born and raised in Colorado, Mary has lived with her family in other parts of the country, but has recently moved back to her home. She says it took fifty years for her to decide what she wanted to be when she grew up...a teddy bear artist! She made her first bears in 1985 and after experimenting with many designs, she gradually started reducing them and now makes miniatures exclusively. In addition to making bears, Mary writes teddy bear poetry and has won Golden Poet awards in 1990 and 1991 from the World of Poetry. She does several shows a year and states that the wonderful people she has met have made a real difference in her life. *Photographs by Reagan Atkinson.*

Angelina
1¾in (5cm) bear made of ultra suede with angel wings and gold plated halo.
INTRODUCED: 1988
ORIGINAL PRICE: $23.00
CURRENT VALUE: $50.00

Cowboy Clint
3in (8cm) bear made in ultra suede, dressed in hat, vest and boots.
INTRODUCED: 1988
ORIGINAL PRICE: $36.00
CURRENT VALUE: $100.00

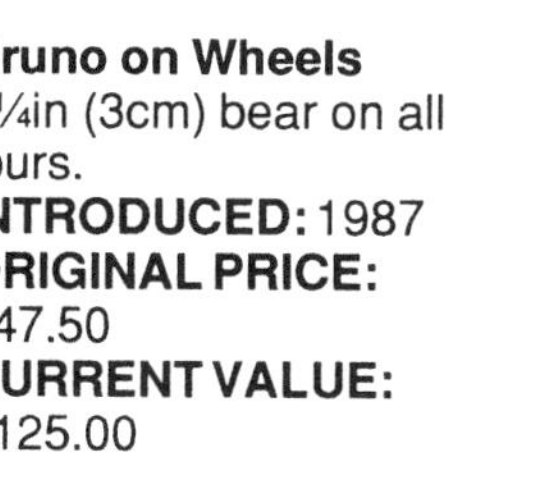

Bruno on Wheels
1¼in (3cm) bear on all fours.
INTRODUCED: 1987
ORIGINAL PRICE: $47.50
CURRENT VALUE: $125.00

BALOUN, SHERRY

7550 N. Milwaukee Avenue
Chicago, Illinois 60648
TRADE NAME: Original Bitte Schoen Bears

Sherry is half of the mother-daughter team of Gigi's Dolls and Sherry's Teddy Bears, and their experience in the doll and bear world originated many years ago. Sherry has been collecting antique and artist bears for a number of years, and started making bears in 1986. Her first effort was a pair of jointed bears specifically dressed for her parents' anniversary. She has since been making bears in acrylic, wools and mohair. Her enjoyment of bear making arises from the excitement of seeing the finishing touches on a bear completed and a personality exemplified. *Photograph by Sherry Baloun.*

Rosealinda
21in (53cm) fully-jointed bear in mohair.
PRODUCTION: 4
ORIGINAL PRICE: $189.00
CURRENT VALUE: $400.00

Simon "Oops"
10in (25cm) tall in brown or white mohair, fully jointed. Originally made as a joke, ***Simon*** appears to have several problems, including cross eyes, pigeon toed stuffing appears to come out at the seams. His motto is "some days are just like that."
INTRODUCED: 1986
PRODUCTION: Limited Edition 150
ORIGINAL PRICE: $45.00
CURRENT VALUE: $175.00

BECK, DORIS

15913 S.E. Eighth Street
Bellevue, Washington 98008
TRADE NAME: Dori's Bears

Doris Beck suspects that she must have been born with a needle in her hand. By the time she was eight, she was busy making doll clothes and then clothing for herself in her early teens. As a registered nurse, she used a needle in a different manner creating bears as gifts and a way of relaxation until the bear making became a business in 1984. Since then Doris has made unclothed bears under the name Dori's Bears, and dressed bears are sold as Couturiere Bear. Many of her bears are one of a kind special orders. *Photographs by Doris Beck.*

Christmas Elves
Third in an annual series of Christmas Bears, they are 13in (33cm) tall in white mohair with red or green mohair body suit. Fully jointed.
INTRODUCED: Christmas 1987
ORIGINAL PRICE: $95.00 each
CURRENT VALUE: $275.00 each

Mr. and Mrs. Santa
Limited edition Christmas bears made for an art gallery in Bellevue, Washington. ***Santa*** is 23in (58cm) tall in tan mohair, fully-jointed. ***Mrs. Santa*** is 22in (56cm) tall in same fabric and construction. Both dressed in red velvet clothing with white acrylic fur trim.
INTRODUCED: Christmas 1988
PRODUCTION: Limited Edition 25 each
ORIGINAL PRICE: $250.00 (***Santa***), $225.00 (***Mrs. Santa***)
CURRENT VALUE: $650.00 (***Santa***), $575.00 (***Mrs. Santa***)

Victorian Carolers
Part of same limited edition group made for art gallery, 17in (43cm) tall, available in tan, white or gray mohair. Dressed in Victorian style outfits with acrylic capes.
INTRODUCED: Christmas 1988
PRODUCTION: Limited Edition 25 each
ORIGINAL PRICE: $225.00 each
CURRENT VALUE: $575.00 each

J. Pierpont Honeyeater
19in (48cm) fully-jointed bear in tipped mohair.
INTRODUCED: 1988
PRODUCTION: Unlimited Production
ORIGINAL PRICE: $145.00
CURRENT VALUE: $350.00

Rosebud
15in (38cm) musical bear in dusty rose distressed mohair. She wears a lace ruff and a butterfly in her ear.
INTRODUCED: 1988
PRODUCTION: Unlimited Production
ORIGINAL PRICE: $125.00
CURRENT VALUE: $300.00

BEDWELL, DEBRA

P.O. Box 511
Northhampton, Massachusetts 01061

TRADE NAME: D'Bears

Debra began her bear making career in 1985. She produced a little rabbit for a friend, and the response was so great from those who saw it, that she took a few orders. She has since sold to some major stores, including Neimann-Marcus and Bloomingdales. Debra uses unusual fabrics, including genuine lambswool, mink and various furs. *Photographs by Debra Bedwell.*

Emily
A fully-jointed bear made of Spanish curly lamb. Various furs and mohair fabrics have also been used.
PRODUCTION: Unlimited Edition
ORIGINAL PRICE: $200.00
CURRENT VALUE: $375.00

Lambswool Bunnies
Originally made of Spanish curly lambswool. Various other lambs wool colors used. Leather lined inner ears, pads and paws.
INTRODUCED: 1987
PRODUCTION: Unlimited Edition
ORIGINAL PRICE: $65.00
CURRENT VALUE: $150.00

The Reagans
A set of these unusual bears went to the White House in 1988. The bears, made in alpaca fabric, are musical. One bear plays "God Bless America" and the other plays the "Star Spangled Banner." Their low price was due to a limitation imposed on gifts to the White House of $150.00 value.
INTRODUCED: 1988
ORIGINAL PRICE: $150.00
CURRENT VALUE: $800.00

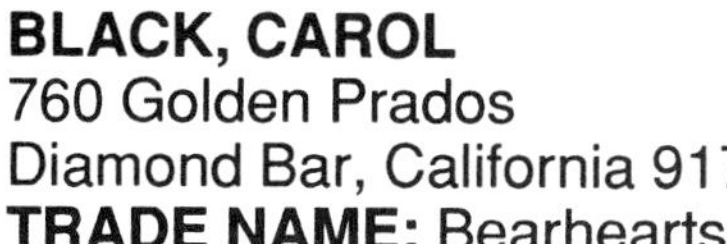

BLACK, CAROL

760 Golden Prados
Diamond Bar, California 91765

TRADE NAME: Bearhearts

Carol's love of teddy bears started nearly forty years ago when a loving father won a three foot brown plush bear for her at the Orange County Fair. In 1983, ten handmade bearobics bears were presented to the Teddy Bear Station in Yorba Linda, and sold over night. Carol has since created many unique and unusual designs, and many have found their way into some famous collections. Carol combines her creative skills with her background in sales, accounting and business. *Photographs by Carol Black.*

Baby Maxine
13in (33cm) bear made in gold alpaca.
INTRODUCED: 1986
PRODUCTION: Limited Edition 50
ORIGINAL PRICE: $150.00
CURRENT VALUE: $425.00

Prima Ballerina
Musical 22in (56cm) teddy plays "Dance Ballerina Dance." Plush fabric. Mauve lace tutu holds potpourri. Porcelain slippers.
INTRODUCED: 1985
PRODUCTION: Limited Edition 100
ORIGINAL PRICE: $250.00
CURRENT VALUE: $825.00

Pierre Bear
13in (33cm) bear made in various color mohair. Head made of paper-mâché, flirty brown eyes made of wood, wooden pink tongue that moves from side to side. Bear has a mouthful of teeth, growler, swivel head and jointed body. Some variation in eyes in some models.
INTRODUCED: 1987
PRODUCTION: Limited Edition 25
ORIGINAL PRICE: $350.00
CURRENT VALUE: $950.00

BLAIR, PATRICIA

4253 Birgit Way
Sacramento, California 95864
TRADE NAME: Blair Bears
Pat, who lives in California with her husband and two children, has been making bears since 1984. A bear made by her mother was the inspiration behind Pat's own talent of creating original patterns for bear making. Pat does all the work on her bears, from cutting to the finished product. *Photograph by Patricia Blair.*

BONNER, JAN

318 Caren Avenue
Worthington, Ohio 43085

TRADE NAME: Bonner Bears and Friends

Jan says it is hard to imagine life without a teddy bear, yet before Christmas 1977 she had never owned a teddy bear. The desire to create a gift for her newborn son inspired her first attempts at bear making. By fall of 1977 she had produced her first bears for sale through friends and craft fairs, and soon local shops and juried art shows were added. By 1983 the business had grown and developed a loyal following of repeat bear customers. Bonner Bears have won numerous awards and can be found in collections throughout the United States, Germany, the United Kingdom, Canada and Australia. *Photographs by Jan Bonner.*

JB Bear
Dense mod-acrylic fur on 13in (33cm) bear.
INTRODUCED: 1987
PRODUCTION: Approximately 75
ORIGINAL PRICE: $42.00
CURRENT VALUE: $100.00

Baby Bear
11in (28cm) fully-jointed bear made in mod-acrylic fur, costumed in blue cotton dress. 4in (10cm) pull toy, non-jointed.
INTRODUCED: 1987
PRODUCTION: Limited Edition 5 sets
ORIGINAL PRICE: $55.00
CURRENT VALUE: $150.00

Downhill Racer
6in (15cm) bear in white wool coating fabric. Button jointed. Sweater sets vary in color.
INTRODUCED: 1987
PRODUCTION: 30 pieces
ORIGINAL PRICE: $45.50
CURRENT VALUE: $125.00

Night-Time Bear
15in (38cm) bear in mod-acrylic fur.
INTRODUCED: 1987
PRODUCTION: 35 pieces
ORIGINAL PRICE: $60.00
CURRENT VALUE: $150.00

Bry
10½in (27cm) fully-jointed teddy in mohair. Leather paws.
INTRODUCED: 1983
PRODUCTION: 6 pieces
ORIGINAL PRICE: $50.00
CURRENT VALUE: $200.00

Flight Into Fantasy
11in (28cm) bear in mod-acrylic fabric. Calico dress with eyelet apron. Goose in mod-acrylic fabric, ultra suede beak with silk flower harness.
INTRODUCED: 1987
ORIGINAL PRICE: $110.00
CURRENT VALUE: $300.00

Jenny's Picnic
15in (38cm) jointed bear in mod-acrylic fur. Dress and pinafore. 5in (13cm) cubs inside picnic basket. Button-jointed movable limbs.
INTRODUCED: 1986
PRODUCTION: 10 sets
ORIGINAL PRICE: $100.00
CURRENT VALUE: $300.00

BRAME, GINGER
7405 Lake Tree Drive
Raleigh, North Carolina 27615
TRADE NAME: The Piece Parade

Ginger fondly remembers her childhood filled with memories of licking the batter from the bowl after helping to make a cake, hearing the screen door slam behind her as she went out to play, and stringing buttons on the floor beside her mom as she sewed. At five years of age, she begged for her first teddy from her eldest sister, and they were never apart thereafter. As a young adult, Ginger survived the North Carolina State School of Design, and somehow all these things have come together to further her career as a teddy bear artist.

Teddy Bear Clown
9½in (24cm) fully-jointed one-of-a-kind bear made in mohair. Costume of tissue lamé decorated with star sequins and tiny gold jingle bells.
INTRODUCED: 1988
ORIGINAL PRICE: $125.00
CURRENT VALUE: $275.00

Enchanted Dolls Limited Edition
Fully-jointed 7½in (19cm) bear in cream tipped mohair, pellet stuffed. Made exclusively for Enchanted Dolls Shop.
INTRODUCED: 1988
PRODUCTION: Limited Edition 20
ORIGINAL PRICE: $50.00
CURRENT VALUE: 125.00

Jack-In-The-Box Bear
Unjointed bear in domestic synthetic. Handmade, hand-painted wooden box with windup music box.
INTRODUCED: 1986
ORIGINAL PRICE: $25.00
CURRENT VALUE: $75.00

BRITTSAN, DEANNA

1155 Uppingham Drive
Thousand Oaks, California 91360

TRADE NAME: Handmade Bears by Deanna Brittsan

Deanna made her first teddy in 1981 from a pattern in a magazine. While she enjoyed the experience, she really wanted to improve. After months of attending shows, practicing pattern designing and observing bear making, Deanna put her first bear together from her own original pattern. Friends and family members encouraged her, so she took them to a local shop where the owner purchased all of them. Deanna started selling to other shops, and participating in shows by entering three of her bears in a contest. Featured are the first, second and third prize bears. Her work has also appeared in magazines. *Photographs by Deanna Brittsan.*

Pebbles
13in (33cm) bear in merino wool. Pellet stuffed.
INTRODUCED: 1987
ORIGINAL PRICE: $95.00
CURRENT VALUE: $250.00

Timmy
10½in (27cm), fully-jointed. Made in llama wool. First place winner.
INTRODUCED: 1986
ORIGINAL PRICE: $90.00
CURRENT VALUE: $275.00

Peter
16in (41cm) bear, fully-jointed. Mohair fabric. Growler. Third place winner.
INTRODUCED: 1986
ORIGINAL PRICE: $130.00
CURRENT VALUE: $400.00

Willy
12in (31cm), fully-jointed. Mohair fabric. Second place winner.
INTRODUCED: 1985
ORIGINAL PRICE: $100.00
CURRENT VALUE: $300.00

BRONZINO, BARBARA and BROWN, JOANN

2349 York Street
East Meadow, New York 11554

TRADE NAME: B & J Originals

Barbara and JoAnn have been working together for over 20 years and both are self-taught in the art of soft sculpture. Their bears range in size from 4in (10cm) to 28in (71cm) tall. Some of the outfits are made from old clothes that have been scaled down to fit the bears. Their character bears are sometimes repeated, but because of the use of old clothing, they are always one-of-a-kind. *Photographs by Tom Bronzino.*

Shoeshine Boy
12in (31cm) fully-jointed bear in synthetic fur. He is dressed in antique shoes, and his clothes and hat are made from old materials. Shoeshine box is made from an old crate.
PRODUCTION: Open Edition
ORIGINAL PRICE: $195.00
CURRENT VALUE: $425.00

Washday Mama and Baby
Mama is 14in (36cm) tall, produced in synthetic fur. Old fabric used for dress. ***Baby*** is 4in (10cm) tall, made in synthetic fur, pellet stuffed.
PRODUCTION: Open Edition
ORIGINAL PRICE: $165.00
CURRENT VALUE: $375.00

Pops and Grandbear
Pops is 17in (43cm) tall, made in mohair. Clothing from old fabrics. ***Grandbear*** is 8in (20cm) tall, made in mohair.
PRODUCTION: Open Edition
ORIGINAL PRICE: $210.00
CURRENT VALUE: $450.00

Honey Color Bear
12in (31cm) bear in distressed mohair. Softy jointed, softy stuffed with pellets and polyester fiberfill. Wears old wool scarf.
INTRODUCED: May 1988
PRODUCTION: Limited Edition 6
ORIGINAL PRICE: $65.00
CURRENT VALUE: $150.00

BROWN, BARBARA
3855 Startouch Drive
Pasadena, California 91107-1341
TRADE NAME: Barbara's Bears
Barbara is the mother of three adult children, a wife and a grandmother. She began making bears in December 1984 as a hobby, and it developed into a full-time business. In the beginning her bears were one-of-a-kind in design but now, because of the number of bears she makes, she no longer feels she has that luxury. Barbara still makes each bear as if she is making it for herself, and she always enjoys the opportunity to meet the people who are buying her bears. *Photograph by Barbara Brown.*

Julius C. Bearmaker
Created in 1988 for the bear competition at Donna Harrison's Baltimore show, this bear won first place. He is 17in (43cm) tall, made from imitation Persian lamb. ***Julius*** has thumbs to hold his needle. Three bears on workbench are low pile fur.
INTRODUCED: 1988
PRODUCTION: Limited Edition 350
ORIGINAL PRICE: $350.00
CURRENT VALUE: $875.00

BUTTITTA, GENIE

942 Brighton
Tonawanda, New York 14150
TRADE NAME: Genie B's Bears
Genie finds creating teddy bears from morning to night very exciting, and not work at all. She has been collecting, restoring and making bears since the late 1970s. She has appeared on local television with new and old bears, and enjoys judging teddy bear contests. Genie recognizes the love and friendship shown by collectors and finds it very rewarding to be a part of it. *Photograph by Elsa Wolf.*

Trashy Teddy
10in (25cm) mohair bear carrying two bags with all her earthly possessions. Dressed in layers of tattered old clothes.
INTRODUCED: 1987
PRODUCTION: Limited Edition 350
ORIGINAL PRICE: $79.99
CURRENT VALUE: $225.00

Wash Day
8½in (22cm) bear made in mohair.
INTRODUCED: 1988
PRODUCTION: Open Edition
ORIGINAL PRICE: $89.00
CURRENT VALUE: $225.00

CALVIN, KAREN AND HOWARD
43501 S.E. Cedar Falls Way
North Bend, Washington 98045
TRADE NAME: Ballard Baines Bears
Karen started making teddy bears as a hobby with two girlfriends in 1979. After three years the other two partners tired of the venture, and just about that time Howard came into the picture. Today their work is widely acclaimed around the world. Living at the base of a mountain near Snoqualmi Pass, they can enjoy wildlife right outside their kitchen window before starting a full day of bear making.

Flossie
This 25in (64cm) bear lady was made to fit antique doll clothes and accessories. Commissioned by Grin and Bear It in Chicago, a series of 12 ***Flossies*** were produced, dressed in clothes suitable for each given month.
INTRODUCED: 1987
PRODUCTION: Limited Edition 12
ORIGINAL PRICE: $1000.00
CURRENT VALUE: $2925.00

Goldsmith
25in (64cm) teddy made in hand-dyed mohair, fully-jointed.
INTRODUCED: 1988
PRODUCTION: Limited Edition 5
ORIGINAL PRICE: $450.00
CURRENT VALUE: $1025.00

Santa Bear
An 18in (46cm) bear in red synthetic, the first in a series of Santas.
INTRODUCED: 1982
PRODUCTION: Approximately 50
ORIGINAL PRICE: $375.00
CURRENT VALUE: $1850.00

Dorian Gray
One of the Calvins' early bears, this 18in (46cm) teddy was made in a gray synthetic fabric. Signed and tagged "Limited Edition designed by H.R. Calvin."
INTRODUCED: 1982
PRODUCTION: Limited Edition 100
ORIGINAL PRICE: $220.00
CURRENT VALUE: $1100.00

King Ludwig
A 20in (51cm) bear in brown or gold synthetic, all numbered and tagged.
INTRODUCED: 1982
PRODUCTION: Numbered Limited Edition 66
ORIGINAL PRICE: $450.00
CURRENT VALUE: $2175.00

Bear and his Friend Grinit
A limited edition made exclusively for Grin and Bear It in Chicago. ***Bear*** is 15in (38cm) made in hand dyed mohair. Fully jointed. ***Dumpster Clown*** is 3½in (9cm).
INTRODUCED: 1988
ORIGINAL PRICE: $325.00
CURRENT VALUE: $850.00

Spencer
Fully-jointed 17in (43cm) teddy in tan mohair.
INTRODUCED: 1988
PRODUCTION: Limited Edition 25
ORIGINAL PRICE: $125.00
CURRENT VALUE: $275.00

Beasley
16in (41cm) jointed bear produced in long, light gold mohair.
INTRODUCED: 1988
PRODUCTION: Open Edition
ORIGINAL PRICE: $110.00
CURRENT VALUE: $225.00

CAVALLERO, CAROL
162 Nortontown Road
Madison, Connecticut 06443
TRADE NAME: Taddy Bears

CHANG, ROSALIND

1980 Spyglass Drive
San Bruno, California 94066
TRADE NAME: Roz Bears
The first bears made by Rosalind were made in 1984 for a friend's wedding cake. Since that time she has continued to make bears so she can add other artist bears to her collection. By day Rosalind is a full-time childrens' librarian, and by night a teddy bear artist. In 1990 Rosalind was honored by *Teddy Bear Review* magazine with a Golden Teddy Award.

Beanie Cap Bear
This 3in (8cm) teddy is fully-jointed, made with mohair fabric. He has a small tail and shaved muzzle. Stuffed with cotton batting. The felt cap has a propeller made of fimo.
INTRODUCED: August 1988
PRODUCTION: Open Edition
ORIGINAL PRICE: $48.00
CURRENT VALUE: $125.00

Precious
16in (41cm) bear in German plush, tinted face, bent arms and legs fully-jointed.
INTRODUCED: 1988 Produced in tan color
PRODUCTION: 101 (discontinued)*
ORIGINAL PRICE: $80.00
CURRENT VALUE: $175.00
*NOTE: A special ***Precious*** was introduced following this bear in cream color and is an open edition.

CLAUSTRE, DONNA

1202 LaBrad Lane
Tampa, Florida 33613
TRADE NAME: Donna Claustre Originals (formerly Original Bucktooth Bears)
As a young college student, Donna's fondest desire was to be a fashion designer, but business college prevailed. After retirement in 1980 she decided to follow her love for designing. Donna does almost all the work on her creations, with some stuffing help from her husband. She feels that "bear folks" are the happiest and nicest people, and they thoroughly enjoy being around them. For Donna and her husband, bears truly mean love.

Country Cousin Bucktooth Bears
(Set of 4) Papa and Mama are 15in (38cm) bears, children 12in (31cm). Made in amerocam plush with tinted faces, leather eyelids and toes.
INTRODUCED: 1984
PRODUCTION: Limited Edition 250 sets
ORIGINAL PRICE: $250.00 set
CURRENT VALUE: $800.00 set

Percival
16in (41cm) bear in German plush, fully-jointed. Signed, dated and numbered on foot.
INTRODUCED: 1987
PRODUCTION: 22
ORIGINAL PRICE: $125.00
CURRENT VALUE: $350.00

Nanny
11in (28cm) bear of wavy caramel mohair, fully-jointed. Some frocks were silk and some were cotton. Handcrafted brass watch and scissors, and a working jumping jack.
INTRODUCED: 1985
PRODUCTION: 51
ORIGINAL PRICE: $190.00
CURRENT VALUE: $675.00

CROWE, NANCY
2400 Woodview Drive
Lansing, Michigan 48911
TRADE NAME: Pearls
Nancy has had a lifelong interest in the field of arts and crafts. In 1985 she designed her first rabbit as a means to stay home with small children. As a result, her exciting new business of producing rabbits and teddy bears under the trade name "Pearls" was born. *Photographs by Kim Kauffman, Photography, Inc.*

Muffin Man
13in (33cm) in wavy caramel mohair, fully-jointed. Jacket, waistcoat, scarf and cap made of silk. Wood tray filled with muffins and breads. Wood and brass hand bell.
INTRODUCED: 1985
PRODUCTION: 95
ORIGINAL PRICE: $190.00
CURRENT VALUE: $675.00

The Peddlar
15in (38cm) fully-jointed bear in mohair. Finely detailed bonnet and shawl. Handmade basket with variety of handmade and antique pieces. Made in two color schemes.
INTRODUCED: 1985
PRODUCTION: 100
ORIGINAL PRICE: $230.00
CURRENT VALUE: $800.00

Katie and Brandon
Each bear 12in (31cm), fully-jointed, mohair. Boy and girl sailor costumes.
INTRODUCED: 1987
PRODUCTION: Limited Edition 10 sets
ORIGINAL PRICE: $245.00 set
CURRENT VALUE: $725.00 set

CUBILLAS, CORLA

8 Burlington Circle
Salinas, California 93906

TRADE NAME: The Dancing Needle

Corla has been designing and creating teddy bears since 1983. She feels she has the best of both worlds, developing a rewarding business and being at home to raise her children. Corla's work has won numerous awards, and she says that each work of art she creates is truly a labor of love. She takes great pride in each bear that comes to life under her "dancing needle" and hopes that one day they will become a well loved antique collectible.

Heywood
14in (36cm) fully-jointed bear in mohair.
INTRODUCED: 1986
PRODUCTION: Open Edition
ORIGINAL PRICE: $125.00
CURRENT VALUE: $375.00

Binkie
13in (33cm) fully-jointed bear in mohair. Paw pads in German merino wool, antique shoe button eyes. Pellet stuffed. Antique eye glasses and book from artist's collection.
INTRODUCED: 1987
PRODUCTION: Open Edition
ORIGINAL PRICE: $135.00
CURRENT VALUE: $375.00

DAHLE, ELIZABETH

9124 E. Arcadia Avenue
San Gabriel, California 91775

TRADE NAME: Liz's Tender Loving Teddies

Liz Dahl has always loved teddy bears, and she especially likes the look of antique teddies. In fact, they have inspired her to design and make teddy bears. Liz lovingly sews each bear completely by hand.

DE PEE, SUZANNE

2208 S. Valley Drive
Visalia, California 93277
TRADE NAME: Honeypot Bears

Suzanne's first Honeypot Bears were created in 1983. She not only created her own unique designs, but started a mail order business to offer designs by other artists as well.

Teddy
21in (53cm) fully-jointed teddy in golden tan merino wool.
INTRODUCED: 1988
PRODUCTION: 4
ORIGINAL PRICE: $70.00
CURRENT VALUE: $150.00

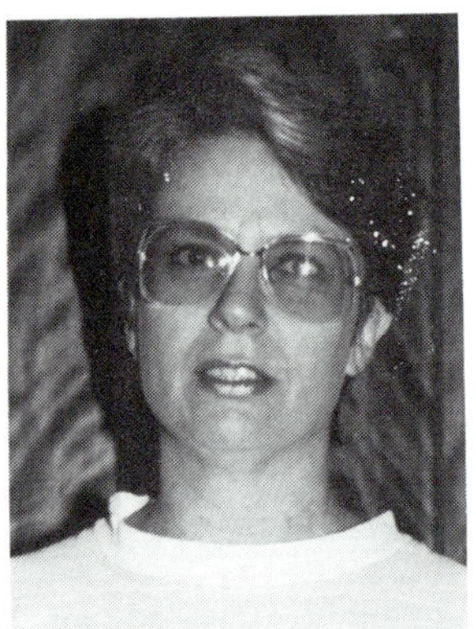

Antoinette
20in (51cm) bear in chestnut color distressed mohair. Hand-dyed pink battenberg lace collar.
INTRODUCED: 1988
PRODUCTION: 7
ORIGINAL PRICE: $195.00
CURRENT VALUE: $475.00

Heather's Bear
9in (23cm) bear in silver-gray alpaca fabric.
INTRODUCED: 1986
PRODUCTION: 25
ORIGINAL PRICE: $65.00
CURRENT VALUE: $200.00

Baby Heidi
9in (23cm) bear in soft, thick German synthetic plush, off-white color. Handwoven cradle basket by Kentucky artist Ann Coleman.
INTRODUCED: 1988
PRODUCTION: 9
ORIGINAL PRICE: $175.00
CURRENT VALUE: $425.00

Geraldine
21in (53cm) girl bear in 1in (3cm) long creamy colored German synthetic plush. Pigskin pads.
INTRODUCED: 1988
PRODUCTION: 17
ORIGINAL PRICE: $200.00
CURRENT VALUE: $500.00

Rebecca
12in (31cm) bear made with distressed mohair. Country dress with detachable collar.
INTRODUCED: 1988
PRODUCTION: Approximately 30
ORIGINAL PRICE: $135.00
CURRENT VALUE: $325.00

DEWIRE, DENISE
27 W. Prospect Street
Ventura, California 93001
TRADE NAME: Bearish Delights
Denise started working with commercial teddy bear patterns in 1985, then quickly turned to designing her own ideas. She makes bears and rabbits using German and English mohair from 6in (15cm) to 25in (64cm) tall. She enjoys dressing bears as jesters, sailors and country kids, and they have won numerous awards.

DICKL, SANDRA
P.O. Box 528
Stroudsburg, Pennsylvania 18360
TRADE NAME: Sankar Bears & Buddies
Teddy bears came into Sandra's life by accident in 1987. She started with a commercial pattern she found, and soon began designing her own little friends and selling them at local craft shows. She finds it exciting to see the faces of the bear collectors when they see her work on display at a show. She continues to do some craft shows as well as bear shows.

Sam
Sandra's first original design is 14in (36cm) tall in antique gold mohair. Fully-jointed. Dressed in hand crocheted vest and bow tie.
INTRODUCED: 1988
ORIGINAL PRICE: $135.00
CURRENT VALUE: $275.00

Petit
This miniature teddy is 2½in (6cm) high, fully-jointed and made with alpaca fabric.
INTRODUCED: 1988
PRODUCTION: 75
ORIGINAL PRICE: $60.00
CURRENT VALUE: $125.00

DIDDIER, DEBORAH
6304 N.W. Pacific Coast Highway
Seal Rock, Oregon 97376
TRADE NAME: Debearahs
Deborah has been making bears for about five years now. She made her first bear for her sister when she was unable to find a very small bear for her sister's doll house. She sold her first bears to a shop in March, 1988 and now sells her bears all over the world. They range in size from ⅝in (2cm) up to 4in (10cm), with most of them 1½in (4cm) or smaller.

DUVALL, DEANNA
1405 Birch Street
Forest Grove, Oregon 97116
TRADE NAME: My Bears & Whimsy
Deanna began designing and making bears in 1978 after becoming enchanted with a friend's extensive teddy collection. She won first place for a bear design in 1982. All of her bears are one-of-a-kind and made entirely by Deanna. Her early bears were in synthetic plush, but since 1985 she has primarily used mohair and other quality materials and supplies. Today they can be found in collections all over the world.

Golden Mohair Bear
This 18in (46cm) mohair teddy is one of ten bears made in this color. A bear from the same pattern was made in plush from 1978-1991.
INTRODUCED: 1988
PRODUCTION: 10
ORIGINAL PRICE (dressed): $120.00
CURRENT VALUE: $225.00

Platform Bear
This 18in (46cm) bear on wheels is made in tan mohair.
INTRODUCED: 1988
PRODUCTION: 6
ORIGINAL PRICE: $150.00
CURRENT VALUE: $350.00

Center Seam Bear
This 29in (74cm) bear is made in yellow mohair, fully-jointed. The two-piece vintage suit is in a pale blue and white stripe. It was also produced in plush from 1978 to 1991.
INTRODUCED: 1987
ORIGINAL PRICE: $215.00 (dressed)
CURRENT VALUE: $575.00

Nutmeg Mohair Bear
This 29in (74cm) teddy is fully-jointed and wears two-piece vintage child's underwear.
INTRODUCED: 1988
PRODUCTION: One-of-a-kind
ORIGINAL PRICE: $235.00
CURRENT VALUE: $575.00

Grand's Bear
Fully-jointed 12in (31cm) bear in mohair. Old shoe button eyes. Sailor collar in flannel. Squeeker.
INTRODUCED: 1988
PRODUCTION: Limited Edition 25
ORIGINAL PRICE: $250.00
CURRENT VALUE: $575.00

DYER, HOLLY

203 Water Street
Mt. Blanchard, Ohio 45867

TRADE NAME: Hollybearys

Holly grew up with the bears in her mother's collection. She made dolls and bears from commercial patterns until her mother (Martha Cramer) designed a bear pattern in 1983, and the bear was actually made by Holly. She does most of the designing and bear making today. Holly's bears are known for their exaggerated humps and perky expressions. In addition to producing bears, Holly enjoys giving bear-making workshops and bear talks. She lives with her husband and two daughters.

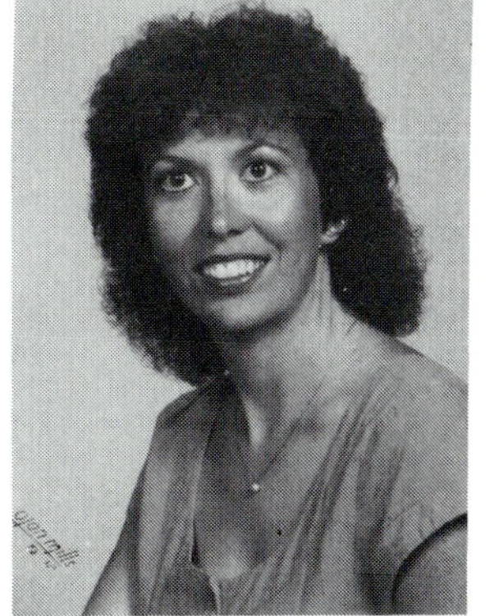

Elvin and Melvin
Fully-jointed 7in (18cm) tall bears. ***Elvin*** is produced in acrylic, ***Melvin*** in mohair.
PRODUCTION: Open Production
ORIGINAL PRICE: $30.00 (***Elvin***); $40.00 (***Melvin***)
CURRENT VALUE: $50.00 (***Elvin***); $75.00 (***Melvin***)

Watersmith
12in (31cm) teddy fully-jointed, made in mohair. Plastic eyes in original design (now made with glass eyes).
INTRODUCED: 1983
PRODUCTION: Open Production
ORIGINAL PRICE: $50.00
CURRENT VALUE: $350.00

J.T.
4in (10cm) teddy in short acrylic, fully-jointed. Hand stitched.
PRODUCTION: Open Production
ORIGINAL PRICE: $25.00
CURRENT VALUE: $125.00

Julyus
7½in (19cm) tall fully-jointed teddy in mohair,
PRODUCTION: Open Production (no longer made)
ORIGINAL PRICE: $40.00
CURRENT VALUE: $100.00

Malcolm
10½in (27cm) tall teddy in mohair. Fully-jointed. Large hump and bent arms.
PRODUCTION: Open Production
ORIGINAL PRICE: $50.00
CURRENT VALUE: $150.00

EGBERT, PAULA

17820 46th Avenue S.
Seattle, Washington 98188
TRADE NAME: Teddy Bear Heaven

Paula Egbert began her bear making adventure in 1983, making bears as gifts for her family. She rarely keeps any of her own bears now, as the excitement for her comes in the creating. Her favorite bear is usually the one she has just finished. She has to plan her bear making activities around the activities of her four children. Paula sewed professionally for a short time for Jantzen Sportswear and now uses that talent in her bear making art.

Bennie
8in (20cm) fully-jointed wool bear with wool jacket and hat.
INTRODUCED: 1988
PRODUCTION: Less than 10
ORIGINAL PRICE: $67.00
CURRENT VALUE: $150.00

Nearly and Dearly
14in (36cm) fully-jointed bears. ***Nearly*** is made in taupe mohair, ***Dearly*** in soft pink hand dyed distressed mohair.
INTRODUCED: 1988
ORIGINAL PRICE: $85.00 each
CURRENT VALUE: $200.00 each

Orion
This 8in (20cm) bear is made in three colors of mohair, adorned with ruffles, sequined trim, bells and a sculpted mask. Fully jointed.
INTRODUCED: 1988
PRODUCTION: 7
ORIGINAL PRICE: $63.00
CURRENT VALUE: $150.00

Bertie
11in (28cm) mohair bear clutching a rocking horse made from an antique quilt.
INTRODUCED: 1987
PRODUCTION: 61
ORIGINAL PRICE: $53.00
CURRENT VALUE: $150.00

Mikey and Molly
Mikey is an 11in (28cm) mohair fully-jointed bear, astride ***Molly***, a 17in (43cm) mohair rocking horse mounted on an oak base.
INTRODUCED: 1987
PRODUCTION: Limited Edition 30
ORIGINAL PRICE: $165.00 Pair
CURRENT VALUE: $450.00 Pair

EGELIN, TATUM

16962 Crestview Court
Victorville, California 92392

Tatum made her first bear in 1984 for her little grandson. For many years prior to that her hobby was collecting vintage clothing, quilts, laces and pieces of beautiful old fabric. This has enabled her to utilize the collection to make and dress her bears. Tatum is limited in her production because she chooses to do all of the work herself. She strives to make each bear perfect.

June Bride
16in (41cm) fully-jointed mohair bear in a dress made of antique lace.
INTRODUCED: 1987 **ORIGINAL PRICE:** $298.00
PRODUCTION: One-of-a-kind **CURRENT VALUE:** $800.00

Sweetheart
An 18in (46cm) fully-jointed bear made in vintage alpaca and an antique baby dress.
INTRODUCED: 1988 **ORIGINAL PRICE:** $169.00
PRODUCTION: Limited Edition 6 **CURRENT VALUE:** $400.00

FICI, PATRICIA

121 Williamstown Way
Columbia, South Carolina 29212
TRADE NAME: Trishka's Treasures
Pat entered the world of bear making when her children were in pre-school several years ago. In fact, her first task was to make a guinea pig. Requests for other animals followed, and the path eventually led to teddy bears. Since she works alone and does all of the designing and bear making, her production is not large. As her work progressed, Pat began to envision her bears as sculptures. Costuming and accessorizing has become an integral part of the final persona of her bears. *Photographs by Patricia Fici.*

Francis of Assisi
Fully-jointed, including knees, allowing him to sit. Hand dyed wavy mohair, growler. 17in (43cm). Dressed in muslin niteshirt and drawers topped with a dark maroon wool tunic and hooded cowl.
INTRODUCED: 1988
PRODUCTION: 4
ORIGINAL PRICE: $350.00
CURRENT VALUE: $900.00

Father Christmas
12in (31cm) bear in alpaca fur, fully-jointed. Bear of angora mohair. Wool knit undergarments with wool felt boots, fully lined red wool overcoat with wool mohair trim.
INTRODUCED: 1985
ORIGINAL PRICE: $225.00
CURRENT VALUE: $775.00

The Seamtress
17in (43cm) fully-jointed bear with special design knees allowing her to sit. Bloomers, slip and cotton dress. Made in gold color mohair. Voice box.
INTRODUCED: 1988
ORIGINAL PRICE: $370.00
CURRENT VALUE: $975.00

Oh What A Face
15in (38cm) fully-jointed bear with growler. Made in cream color mohair. Hand-painted glass eyes. Dressed in a pinafore.
INTRODUCED: 1987
PRODUCTION: 16
ORIGINAL PRICE: $170.00
CURRENT VALUE: $500.00

Navy Ensign
15in (38cm) fully-jointed bear in full uniform of a Navy Ensign.
INTRODUCED: 1987
PRODUCTION: 2
ORIGINAL PRICE: $350.00
CURRENT VALUE: $1000.00

Raleigh and Molly
8½in (22cm) wavy wool bears, fully-jointed. Wearing sailor outfits.
INTRODUCED: 1987
PRODUCTION: 6
ORIGINAL PRICE: $55.00 (***Raleigh***); $65.00 (***Molly***)
CURRENT VALUE: $150.00 (***Raleigh***); $175.00 (***Molly***):

FLEMING, SANDY

53580 Mendoza Avenue
La Quinta, California 92253

TRADE NAME: Sandy Fleming Bears

Sandy's bear making career began with a teddy bear making class at a local craft shop. She made two additional bears the next day and has not stopped since. She has a strong background in creative arts, including doll making and quilting, painting, drawing and sewing. In addition to making bears, Sandy enjoys doing teddy bear shows and going to conferences.

Bunny Bear
Miniature 1¾in (5cm) bear made of ultra suede. Hand stitched. Wearing bunny outfits.
INTRODUCED: 1987
PRODUCTION: 6
ORIGINAL PRICE: $60.00
CURRENT VALUE: $175.00

Babycake
Miniature 1¾in (5cm) bear, hand stitched in ultra suede. Wearing bunny slippers.
INTRODUCED: 1987
PRODUCTION: 8
ORIGINAL PRICE: $80.00
CURRENT VALUE: $200.00

Beggar T. Bear, Blossom Wine, Blossom, Woody
All four bears are 10½in (27cm) tall, made in synthetic fabric.
INTRODUCED: 1987
PRODUCTION: Varies up to 35
ORIGINAL PRICE: $45.00
CURRENT VALUE: $125.00

Lee Series Bears (Peggy Lee, General Lee, Robert E. Lee)
All bears are 8½in (22cm) high, fully-jointed. ***General Lee*** in golden tan wavy wool, ***Peggy Lee*** in off-white mohair, ***Robert E.*** in gold mohair.
INTRODUCED: 1987
PRODUCTION: Varies up to 20
ORIGINAL PRICE: $45.00
CURRENT VALUE: $125.00

Teddy Roosevelt Saving the Cub
14in (36cm) ***Teddy Roosevelt*** with 8½in (22cm) cub. Made in distressed mohair, old army coat felt uniform. ***Cub*** has open mouth and two-toned muzzle.
INTRODUCED: 1988
ORIGINAL PRICE: $235.00 Set
CURRENT VALUE: $575.00 Set

Jester Lee
8½in (22cm) fully-jointed bear in gold mohair and maroon upholstery fabric.
INTRODUCED: 1987
PRODUCTION: 6
ORIGINAL PRICE: $65.00
CURRENT VALUE: $175.00

FOSKEY, SUE AND RANDALL
Rt. #1, Box 68
Ocean View, Delaware 19970
TRADE NAME: Nostalgic Bear Co.
This very active couple are well-known throughout our business. Sue and Randall began their business in 1983 and are kept very busy showing at numerous teddy bear and doll shows throughout the country, including the New York Toy Fair. They supply over 125 shops throughout this country, and in Canada, Germany, England and Holland. In addition to handcrafting bears and their marketing activities, the Foskeys do workshops at conventions, give seminars, and make convention souvenirs. They have won numerous awards for their design and workmanship and have appeared on television and been featured in newspapers.
Photographs by Randall Foskey.

Casey and Quackers
10in (25cm) fully-jointed bear in light caramel mohair. Wears red felt baseball cap and red bow. Duck is made in white mohair with orange-yellow felt beak and feet. Squeeker in tummy.
INTRODUCED: 1988
PRODUCTION: Limited Edition, Signed and Numbered
ORIGINAL PRICE: $75.00 set
CURRENT VALUE: $200.00 set

Hartford
10in (25cm) mohair jointed bear designed and produced for country entertainer John Hartford to be sold at his road appearances. Arms designed to hold and strum banjo. Plastic banjo.
INTRODUCED: 1987
PRODUCTION: Limited Edition 50, Signed and Numbered
ORIGINAL PRICE: $60.00
CURRENT VALUE: $175.00

The Money Bear
Shoulder purse with opening under head. Head has growler to make bear growl when purse is opened and closed. First purses produced in acrylic plush with teddy bear print cotton fabric liner. Later production in mohair, various liner fabric.
INTRODUCED: 1987
PRODUCTION: Open
ORIGINAL PRICE:: $45.00 (Acrylic Plush); $60.00 (Mohair)
CURRENT VALUE: $100.00 (Acrylic Plush); $150.00 (Mohair)

Suzi No-No
9½in (24cm) rusty brown mohair fully-jointed bear. Wears lace collar with satin rose. Tail moves head to say "No." Signed and numbered. No mouth.
INTRODUCED: 1986 for Valentines Day
PRODUCTION: Limited Edition 100
ORIGINAL PRICE: $42.00
CURRENT VALUE: $125.00

William
11in (28cm) fully-jointed teddy produced in off-white merino wool. Also produced in 21in (53cm) size.
INTRODUCED: 1987
PRODUCTION: Limited Edition 50 pieces in 11in; 25 pieces in 21in
ORIGINAL PRICE: $50.00 (11in); $195.00 (21in)
CURRENT VALUE: $125.00 (11in); $350.00 (21in)

Nostalgic Bear
This 12in (31cm) fully-jointed bear is the Foskey's first copyrighted design. It is made in champagne mohair and wears a brown velvet Lord Fauntleroy hat. Girl bears in this design wore a Kate Greenaway hat. It was also made in gray mohair. Earlier bears had suede-like paw pads, later replaced by felt. Also produced in 14in (36cm) size.
PRODUCTION: Limited Edition 100
ORIGINAL PRICE: $55.00 (12in); $75.00 (14in)
CURRENT VALUE: $200.00 (12in); $250.00 (14in)

Barri Christmas
19in (48cm) fully-jointed bear in blonde white mohair. White leather pads. Tags numbered.
INTRODUCED: 1987
PRODUCTION: Limited Edition 30
ORIGINAL PRICE: $220.00
CURRENT VALUE: $600.00

FRANKS, GLORIA

Rt. #1, Box 221-B
Walker, West Virginia 26180

TRADE NAME: Goose Creek

Gloria started making teddy bears in the mid 1980s, having produced dolls before that. She works almost exclusively in mohair now, and dresses many of her bears in country or Victorian costumes. She markets primarily through stores so that she can stay home and enjoy the peace and quiet of her country home. She shares her home with her husband, peacocks, geese, ducks, two cats and four dogs. *Photographs by Mike Franks.*

Abbearlonia
14in (36cm) fully-jointed bear in blonde mohair. Blue glass eyes.
INTRODUCED: 1985
PRODUCTION: 58
ORIGINAL PRICE: $80.00
CURRENT VALUE: $275.00

Petula
13in (33cm) bear in rose and white mohair. Fully-jointed.
INTRODUCED: 1987
PRODUCTION: 37
ORIGINAL PRICE: $94.00
CURRENT VALUE: $250.00

The Freeman Intellectual Bear
16in (41cm) fully-jointed bear in synthetic plush. Handmade wire glasses.
INTRODUCED: 1984 (pictured with smaller 13in [33cm] Freeman bear).
PRODUCTION: 300
ORIGINAL PRICE: $69.00
CURRENT VALUE: $250.00

Freeman Bear Family
Three fully-jointed acrylic plush bears in 10in (25cm), 13in (33cm) and 16in (41cm) size.
INTRODUCED: 1984
PRODUCTION: 250
ORIGINAL PRICE: $49.00 (10in); $59.00 (13in); $69.00 (116in)
CURRENT VALUE: $175.00 (10in); $200.00 (13in); $250.00 (16in)

FREEMAN, CHESTER

398 S. Main St.
Geneva, New York 14456-2614

Chester Freeman is a former college chaplain from the University of Massachusetts and Amherst College. He began his career as a teddy bear artist in the early 1980s. He believes that teddy bears are a symbol of his spirituality. He is a graduate of Hampton University with a master's degree in theology from Colgate Rochester Divinity School/ Bexley Hall/Crozer Theological Seminary in Rochester, New York. After leaving his chaplaincy, Chester pursued his interest in the arts. When not working on his teddy bears, you may find him serving as a fine arts agent and international correspondent for the *Textile Fibre Forum Magazine* of Mittagong, Australia.

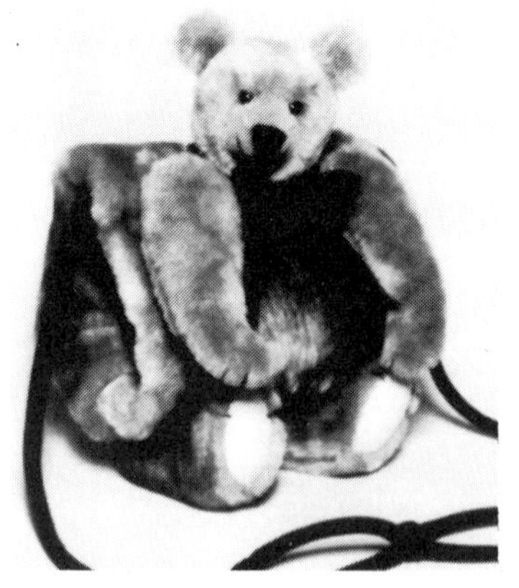

Freeman Bear Muff
Made in acrylic plush in both child and adult size. Jointed head. Velvet cording.
ORIGINAL PRICE: $89.00
CURRENT VALUE: $350.00

Ole the Norwegian Jester
A 4½in (12cm) fully-jointed bear in hand-dyed alpaca. Lace collar.
INTRODUCED: 1988
PRODUCTION: Limited Edition 25
ORIGINAL PRICE: $115.00
CURRENT VALUE: $275.00

FRISCHMANN, ROSALIE

Rt. #1, Box 70-A
Arena, Wisconsin 53503
TRADE NAME: Mill Creek Creations

Since 1983 Rosalie Frischmann has been creating her charming animals under the Mill Creek Creations label. The first bears were made as gifts for her small daughters. Soon her hobby blossomed into a thriving business. While Rosalie enjoys the design and creation of her bears, the greatest reward comes from the pleasure they bring to her many collectors.

Blueberry
6½in (17cm) tall bear in hand-dyed mohair. She wears a light blue rose in left ear.
INTRODUCED: 1986
PRODUCTION: 85
ORIGINAL PRICE: $50.00
CURRENT VALUE: $150.00

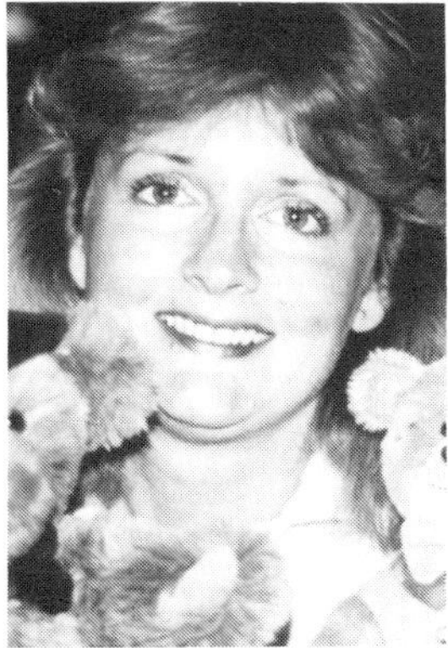

GADANO, JEAN AND FRY, MITZI
P.O. Box 18145
San Jose, California 95158
TRADE NAME: Tabby's Bears
This mother-daughter partnership began in 1984. Jean does the buying of supplies, and designs and makes many of the bears. She also does the photography. Mitzi also has a hand in creating. In fact she did most of the designing of the Bitzi Bear which won a blue ribbon at the 1987 A.T.B.A.G. conference. She also makes all the clothes and accessories for the bears.
Photographs by Jean Gadano.

Bitzi Bear
12in (31cm) tall, fully-jointed. Produced in tan mohair. Wears heavy lace collar and ribbon. Designed with bent leg.
INTRODUCED: 1987
PRODUCTION: 10
ORIGINAL PRICE: $95.00
CURRENT VALUE: $275.00

Gilbert
20in (51cm) tall, fully-jointed. Designed by Jean Gadano as a turn-of-the-century school boy bear. Outfit by Mitzi Fry. Wool tweed knickers and hat, cotton shirt, bow tie and stockings. Wears antique baby shoes and antique glasses.
INTRODUCED: 1989
PRODUCTION: Open Edition
ORIGINAL PRICE: $355.00
CURRENT VALUE: $825.00

Cubby
A fully-jointed miniature teddy measuring 2¾in (7cm). Made in mohair.
INTRODUCED: 1985
PRODUCTION: Open Edition
ORIGINAL PRICE: $60.00
CURRENT VALUE: $200.00

GAMBLE, ELAINE FUJITA

9510 232nd S.W.
Edmonds, Washington 98020

TRADE NAME: Fujita-Gamble Teddies

Elaine's teddy bear collecting started a number of years ago when a friend gave her a bear as a gift. She collects antique teddies, artist made and commercial bears but is widely known for her remarkable miniature bears. Elaine is a full-time physical education specialist, so her bear making time is somewhat limited. She markets her bears at shows only and personally enjoys meeting the people who collect her bears.

Pockets
This tiny ¾in (2cm) tall teddy was made to fit in an antique pocket watch case. Fully jointed.
INTRODUCED: 1986
PRODUCTION: Open Edition
ORIGINAL PRICE: $110.00
CURRENT VALUE: $350.00

Molly and Bunny
4in (10cm) mohair fully-jointed teddy. Dressed in old handkerchief dress. ***Bunny*** is 2in (5cm) tall, fully-jointed.
INTRODUCED: 1988
ORIGINAL PRICE: $65.00 (***Molly***); $50.00 (***Bunny***)
CURRENT VALUE: $175.00 (***Molly***); $125.00 (***Bunny***)

GARD, DIANE

1005 West Oak St.
Fort Collins, Colorado 80521

TRADE NAME: Diane Gard Enterprises

Since 1982 the whimsical, quizzical-eyed bears with a heart have been created by Colorado artist Diane Gard. Diane often uses unusual vintage fabrics to create unique, charming bears. This award-winning artist also designs bears with a less traditional look, adapting her old patterns to innovative new styles, yet retaining the most endearing qualities of the teddy bear. On the chest of each bear is a glass heart that has become Diane's trademark, and which symbolizes the love she brings to her work.

Maxwell
19in (48cm) fully-jointed teddy in golden color mohair tipped in rich brown. Shaved muzzle, paws and feet pads. ***Maxwell*** has received many artistic awards, and was featured on the cover of the **Teddy Bear Artist Annual**.
INTRODUCED: 1987
PRODUCTION: 200
ORIGINAL PRICE: $200.00
CURRENT VALUE: $550.00

Rough Rider
15in (38cm) bear of unusual vintage mohair fabric used by the Pierce Arrow Motor Company to upholster automobiles. Produced as a tribute to Teddy Roosevelt's Rough Riders Volunteer Calvary.
INTRODUCED: 1986
PRODUCTION: 250
ORIGINAL PRICE: $150.00
CURRENT VALUE: $475.00

Mrs. Rough Rider
Created as a companion piece to ***Rough Rider bear***, each one is named for a wife of a member of the volunteer calvary. 15in (38cm), fully jointed. Vintage upholstery mohair fabric.
INTRODUCED: 1988
PRODUCTION: 75
ORIGINAL PRICE: $175.00
CURRENT VALUE: $475.00

Jester Bears
10½in (27cm) tall, fully-jointed bears made in distressed mohair with different color upholstery mohair bodies.
PRODUCTION: 50
ORIGINAL PRICE: $75.00
CURRENT VALUE: $175.00

GATTO, LYNN

59 Jones Rd.
Wallingford, Connecticut 06492
TRADE NAME: Limerick Bear Inc.

Like many other bear artists, Lynn started out making a wide variety of crafts which she sold at local shows. She quickly noticed that her teddies were always the best selling items on her table, so she decided to try her hand at designing her own patterns. She signed up for her first show in 1985. In the beginning her family thought it was all for fun, but after a few successful shows they realized that Lynn had her own small business in full bloom. Now her husband Phil helps trace her patterns on mohair and cuts them out for her. Both share in the jointing, and Lynn does the stuffing, sewing and finishing. Her business has taken them to many different parts of the United States and to England.

Franklin
11in (28cm) fully-jointed teddy in mohair. Hand distressed wool paw pads. Cedar excelsior stuffing.
PRODUCTION: 50
ORIGINAL PRICE: $75.00
CURRENT VALUE: $175.00

Bellhop Teddy Bear
Fully-jointed 19in (48cm) teddy in distressed mohair for head, upholstery red and black mohair for body, arms and legs.
PRODUCTION: 4
ORIGINAL PRICE: $185.00
CURRENT VALUE: $450.00

GILL, PATRICIA

512 Campbell Acres
Cleveland, Texas 77327
TRADE NAME: Woodhaven Cottage

Pat's bear making career started in 1986, but her sewing skills can be traced to the age of nine, when she sewed on her mother's old treadle machine. In fact, she used to design and make her own toys. Her husband and three children are very supportive and inspiring to her. She hopes to someday design and produce bears full time, but right now she shares her time with home schooling the children, running a household and church activities.

Shebearazod
11in (28cm) bear, arms and legs jointed. Harem bear wears a removable veil, a diamond in her belly button, a ring on her finger, a bell on her toes and a gold earring in her ear. Synthetic plush. Produced exclusively for Bear-in-Mind.
INTRODUCED: 1987
PRODUCTION: Limited Edition 50
ORIGINAL PRICE: $50.00
CURRENT VALUE: $100.00

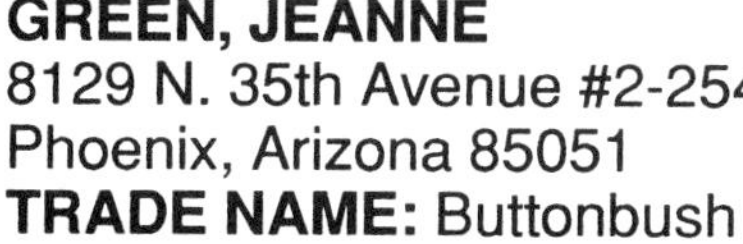

GREEN, JEANNE
8129 N. 35th Avenue #2-254
Phoenix, Arizona 85051
TRADE NAME: Buttonbush

Jean discovered her first jointed teddy bear at a neighbor's sale in 1984. She was already skilled in a variety of crafting and sewing mediums, and teddy bears captured her heart. She spent every spare moment designing and stitching, with visions of another unique bear urging her to create just one more. Over the years, Jeanne has come to realize just how important original fabric and fur soft sculptures are to collectors worldwide. For her, the ultimate reward would be to know that her work could, after generations of loving hugs, still lend a comforting paw, a listening ear, or coax a smile to the lips of some unsuspecting human being. *Photographs by Olan Mills, Inc.*

Bride and Groom
18in (46cm) fully-jointed bears in upholstery fabric.
INTRODUCED: 1986
PRODUCTION: One of a kind set
ORIGINAL PRICE: $130.00
CURRENT VALUE: $375.00

Button Big Bear
21in (53cm) fully-jointed bear in 1in (3cm) black plush (first 25 in domestic plush, last 17 in imported German plush).
INTRODUCED: 1987
PRODUCTION: 42
ORIGINAL PRICE: $140.00
CURRENT VALUE: $375.00

Charlie
10in (25cm) fully-jointed bear in mohair.
INTRODUCED: 1988
PRODUCTION: 2
ORIGINAL PRICE: $69.00
CURRENT VALUE: $150.00

Baby Buttonbush Bear
16in (41cm) fully-jointed bear in mohair.
INTRODUCED: 1988
PRODUCTION: One-of-a-kind
ORIGINAL PRICE: $135.00
CURRENT VALUE: $300.00

Honey Bear
14in (36cm) fully-jointed bear in domestic plush, wearing sweater and cap.
INTRODUCED: 1987
PRODUCTION: One-of-a-kind
ORIGINAL PRICE: $45.00
CURRENT VALUE: $100.00

Bear Footed Silly Sleeper
14in (36cm) fully-jointed bear in domestic plush.
INTRODUCED: 1987
PRODUCTION: One-of-a-kind
ORIGINAL PRICE: $40.00
CURRENT VALUE: $100.00

Ted E. Hug Activity Bear
Non-jointed 18in (46cm) bear in upholstery fabric, safety eyes.
INTRODUCED: 1987
PRODUCTION: One-of-a-kind
ORIGINAL PRICE: $30.00
CURRENT VALUE: $75.00

HAGGARD, MARY

1304 Helen Avenue
Terre Haute, Indiana 47802
TRADE NAME: Haggard Huggables

Mary Haggard is a dual talent, internationally recognized for her paintings of Arabian horses, and since 1986 she has added teddy bear artist to her talents. She originally added the bear making to take up some of her spare time, but the demand for her bears keeps her so busy she now has to work in time for her painting. *Photographs by Mary Haggard.*

Jasper
23in (58cm) bear in black synthetic fur with tan shaded muzzle, tan eye spots, growler. Hand-shaped vinyl nose. Signed and numbered.
INTRODUCED: 1988
PRODUCTION: Limited Edition 20
ORIGINAL PRICE: $225.00
CURRENT VALUE: $475.00

Dumpling
10½in (27cm) bear in soft synthetic fur. Fully jointed. Wears a polka dot bow with blue heart wooden name tag.
INTRODUCED: 1988
ORIGINAL PRICE: $90.00
CURRENT VALUE: $200.00

Haggard Cubbies IV
These 15in (38cm) bears were offered in a choice of Black Bear, Kodiak, Grizzly and Polar bear. Three quarters of the limited edition were black bears. Fully jointed, domestic plush. Black safety eyes, hand-shaped vinyl noses. Suede paws with defined toes. Each bear has name painted on wooden tag.
INTRODUCED: 1987
PRODUCTION: Limited Edition 100
ORIGINAL PRICE: $115.00
CURRENT VALUE: $275.00

HAHN, LILLIAN

626 E. Main St.
Jackson, Missouri 63755
TRADE NAME: The Bear House
Lillian Hahn is now in a second career, having retired after 40 years as supervisor and instructor in a large factory. She began bear making in 1985 and now has 17 styles she has created, working mostly with mohair.

Jonathan
16in (41cm) fully-jointed teddy, stuffed with polyfil or pellets.
ORIGINAL PRICE: $150.00
CURRENT VALUE: $300.00

Munchkins
10in (25cm) fully-jointed teddy in tipped mohair with pellet stuffing. Wears either handknit sweater and cap, or lace, ribbon and flower collar.
INTRODUCED: 1988
PRODUCTION: Open
ORIGINAL PRICE: $130.00
CURRENT VALUE: $300.00

HARRELL, SERIETA

10590 Vista Lago Pl.
San Diego, California 92131
TRADE NAME: Sersha Collectibles
After working as head designer for a major manufacturer, the love and the lure of the teddy bear and a desire for more creative freedom led Serieta to devote her talent to her own business. She produces all bears, bunnies and kittens by herself. She has won numerous first place awards at major shows, but just knowing her creations are loved by collectors is her best award of all.

HARRISON, DICKIE

707 Maiden Choice Ln. #8202
Baltimore, Maryland 21228

In 1982 at age 65, Dickie was preparing to retire after 25 years in the insurance industry. She was looking for a new hobby, having been a miniature enthusiast for years, crafting doll house furniture and dolls. Her daughter Donna Harrison West (promoter of the popular Baltimore Convention and shows) had just become involved with teddy bears and challenged her mother to make a little bear. It was a challenge Dickie could not refuse! At that time there were relatively few artists making miniature bears, and Dickie's incredible little teddies became very popular. I remember the first time Doris and I met Dickie at the Teddy Tribune Convention perhaps nine years ago, and we were absolutely in awe of her work. Needless to say, our collection now includes a fair number of her bears. Soon Dickie was hearing from collectors all over the world. Dickie says she never had more fun or met nicer people, but unfortunately she stopped making miniature bears in 1989 when her hands and eyes began to fail her.

Button Bears
Some of Dickie's early bears in 2in (5cm) and 3in (8cm) size. Note quarter in lower center of photograph for size comparison. Button jointed.
INTRODUCED: 1982
PRODUCTION: 100
ORIGINAL PRICE: $45.00
CURRENT VALUE: $225.00

Standard 3in (8cm) Bear
Fully jointed, 3in (8cm) tall
INTRODUCED: 1984
PRODUCTION: 150
ORIGINAL PRICE: $65.00
CURRENT VALUE: $225.00

Bell Hop
Fully-jointed miniature Bell Hop. Costume is part of body.
PRODUCTION: Limited Edition 50
ORIGINAL PRICE: $70.00
CURRENT VALUE: $275.00

Abner and Popcorn
Abner is a fully-jointed, center seam miniature. ***Popcorn*** is a head jointed pull toy on wheels.
INTRODUCED: 1984
PRODUCTION: Limited Edition 50 each
ORIGINAL PRICE: $65.00 each
CURRENT VALUE: $250.00 each

Teddy B and Teddy G
Miniature plush version of the literary characters from the 1920s.
INTRODUCED: 1984
PRODUCTION: Limited Edition 50 sets
ORIGINAL PRICE: $150.00 pair
CURRENT VALUE: $600.00 pair

Jester
3in (8cm) Jester bear. Outfit is part of body.
INTRODUCED: 1985
PRODUCTION: Limited Edition 50
ORIGINAL PRICE: $70.00
CURRENT VALUE: $250.00

Yes-No Bear
3in (8cm) mechanical bear with head movement in yes-no direction, controlled by moving tail.
INTRODUCED: 1985
PRODUCTION: Limited Edition 6
ORIGINAL PRICE: $65.00
CURRENT VALUE: $225.00

Buckshot
Fully-jointed miniature, "stuffed" with buckshot, making him very poseable.
INTRODUCED: 1987
PRODUCTION: Limited 25
ORIGINAL PRICE: $75.00
CURRENT VALUE: $175.00

HAUGHT, RHONDA

P.O. Box 25
Fairview, West Virginia 26570
TRADE NAME: Maul and Paw

Unable to find a quality old-fashioned bear at home, Rhonda produced her own. Designing her first bear ignited her passion for bears. Through the years she received a great deal of help from her husband Stan and from her sister-in-law Cathie Haught.

Ezekiel
Poseable jointed 24in (61cm) teddy produced in wavy mohair with center seam head.
PRODUCTION: Limited Edition 50
ORIGINAL PRICE: $195.00
CURRENT VALUE: $450.00

Victoria
18in (46cm) fully-jointed bear in mohair. Mink hat and collar.
INTRODUCED: 1987
PRODUCTION: One-of-a-kind
ORIGINAL PRICE: $175.00
CURRENT VALUE: $425.00

HAYES, TERRY

2447 Skidmore Rd.
Greensburg, Pennsylvania 15601
TRADE NAME: Pendelton's Teddy Bears
Terry worked in Nuclear Medicine for seven years, then decided to stay home with her children. She started her bear making career in 1983, working in acrylic fur with commercial patterns. She expected to sell them for children to play with, but discovered that adults were collecting them. One of her teddies sold at a teddy bear auction in 1985 for nearly six times the price she had sold them for, so she purchased her first yard of mohair at that same show.

Bride Bear
18in (46cm) fully-jointed bear produced in pink mohair.
INTRODUCED: 1988
PRODUCTION: One-of-a-kind
ORIGINAL PRICE: $115.00
CURRENT VALUE: $275.00

Prez's Teddy Bear
This 18in (46cm) fully-jointed teddy was designed as an Inaugural gift for President Bush. German synthetic.
INTRODUCED: 1988
PRODUCTION: 3
ORIGINAL PRICE: $175.00
CURRENT VALUE: $400.00

HENDERSON, BILLEE

9312 Santayana Dr.
Fairfax, Virginia 22031

Billee has spent many years sewing for herself, her five children and producing gifts for others. She graduated from the University of Maryland with a major in clothing and textile. She produced her first jointed bear in 1984 for a son born in Scotland, and with it was born a "bear obsession" that continues with more ideas than time. *Photographs by Nancy Bamford Photography.*

Mary Ann
19in (48cm) fully-jointed bear produced in pale yellow mohair. Crocheted dress.
INTRODUCED: 1988
PRODUCTION: 40
ORIGINAL PRICE: $175.00
CURRENT VALUE: $425.00

Bearnard
17in (43cm) mohair bear wearing a beret and holding a violin.
INTRODUCED: 1986
PRODUCTION: 10
ORIGINAL PRICE: $95.00
CURRENT VALUE: $300.00

HENRY, MIKE AND LINDA

4 Beck St.
Canal Winchester, Ohio 43110
TRADE NAME: Bearloom Bears

Linda and Mike have backgrounds well suited to their teddy bear business. Linda studied at Kent State University and the Columbus College of Art and Design and is a freelance commercial artist. Mike, who also attended the Columbus College of Art and Design, has extensive training in fine art, design and cartooning. The Henrys are interested in quality rather than quantity, so each bear produced is carefully researched before the first stitch is made. Linda does the majority of the machine work, while Mike enjoys giving each bear its own unique personality in hand finishing. The creative force behind the clothing and accessories is Mike's mother Barb Henry. *Photographs by Linda Henry.*

Marcy And Marty Maritimus
15in (38cm) bears produced in acrylic fur with black leather paw pads and noses. Bride and groom pair.
INTRODUCED: 1988
PRODUCTION: One-of-a-kind set
ORIGINAL PRICE: $200.00 pair
CURRENT VALUE: $500.00 pair

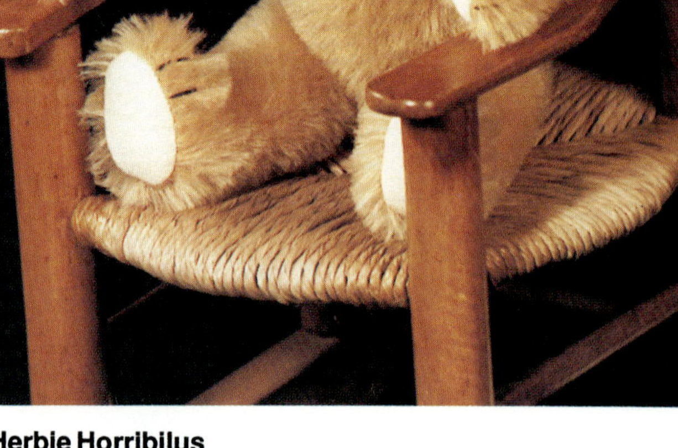

Herbie Horribilus
9in (23cm) fully-jointed teddy in gold mohair.
INTRODUCED: 1988
PRODUCTION: 5
ORIGINAL PRICE: $75.00
CURRENT VALUE: $175.00

Bunny Bears
14in (36cm) bear in acrylic fur. Straw bonnet adorned with silk flowers and bunny ears.
INTRODUCED: 1988
PRODUCTION: Limited Edition 25
ORIGINAL PRICE: $75.00
CURRENT VALUE: $175.00

Black Bart
17in (43cm) fully-jointed bear in domestic plush.
INTRODUCED: 1988
PRODUCTION: 50
ORIGINAL PRICE: $50.00
CURRENT VALUE: $200.00

Mr. Peabody
18in (46cm) bear in gold wavy wool. Gold wire rim glasses, buttoned-down oxford collar and red paisley bow tie.
INTRODUCED: 1988
PRODUCTION: Limited Edition 25
ORIGINAL PRICE: $90.00
CURRENT VALUE: $225.00

Bettina
20in (51cm) bear in European plush with porcelain face.
INTRODUCED: 1988
PRODUCTION: Limited Edition 1000
ORIGINAL PRICE: $495.00
CURRENT VALUE: $1450.00

Little Lost Bears
Fully-jointed 9in (23cm) bear in mohair.
INTRODUCED: 1988
PRODUCTION: 50
ORIGINAL PRICE: $110.00
CURRENT VALUE: $275.00

HILGENDORF, BETSY
P.O. Box 1266
Phantom Ranch
Grand Canyon, Arizona 86023
TRADE NAME: Purple Crayon Creations

If an artist is inspired by their surroundings, Betsy Hilgendorf has to be one of the most inspired artists in the country, living right at the bottom of the Grand Canyon! Easy errands for most of us became huge projects for this bear maker. Betsy took a sewing class in high school, and while everyone else was making a dress, Betsy produced her first bear. The incident was far more significant than she realized at the time. She continued to make bears, but it was not until 1984 that she officially formed Purple Crayon Creations, and she says it gave her the best excuse to travel she has ever had.

Pink and Grey Bears
10in (25cm) bears in light pink or gray mohair, fully jointed. Cotterpin fastened wooden joints.
ORIGINAL PRICE: $72.00
CURRENT VALUE: $150.00

Tipped Mohair Bear
10in (25cm) fully-jointed bear in tipped mohair. Bolt and locknut fastened wooden joints.
ORIGINAL PRICE: $90.00
CURRENT VALUE: $200.00

HINES, DEBORAH AND DERIK

3271 March Terrace
Cincinnati, Ohio 45239

TRADE NAME: Teddy Bear Blessings

This minister and wife combination discovered collector teddy bears in the early 1980s, but with a family of five children to raise they could not afford the top quality bears, so they teamed up to design and produce their own. Their teddies soon started to inhabit other homes as well, and their small but thoroughly enjoyable bear business was born.

Bethany and Aaron
Fully-jointed 9in (23cm) teddies in acrylic plush. (Now produced in mohair).
INTRODUCED: 1987
PRODUCTION: 12
ORIGINAL PRICE: $22.00 each
CURRENT VALUE: $50.00 each

Cissie
15in (38cm) fully-jointed bear in tan acrylic plush.
PRODUCTION: One-of-a-kind
ORIGINAL PRICE: $35.00
CURRENT VALUE: $75.00

Elfabear and Elfie
17½in (45cm) fully-jointed mohair bear. Red velvet and gold lamé tunic lined in taffeta plaid. Dark green velvet pants, green felt cap, leather boots. ***Elfie*** is a 6in (15cm) fully-jointed bear in gold mohair.
INTRODUCED: 1986
PRODUCTION: Limited Edition 12
ORIGINAL PRICE: $495.00 set
CURRENT VALUE: $1600.00 set

HOCKENBERRY, DEE

14191 Bacon Rd.
Albion, New York 14411

Dee Hockenberry has been designing and making bears for over ten years. Her bears may be found in shops across the United States, England and Japan. Although she occasionally makes issues of 25 or more for a few select catalogues, she prefers to design and execute one-of-a-kind teddies. Along with her photographer husband, Tom, she is the author of several teddy bear books, including a price guide, published by Hobby House Press, Inc. and is a contributor to *Teddy Bear and friends®* magazine. Dee is also a dealer in vintage teddies and other soft toys with partner Lorraine Oakley. *Photograph by Tom Hockenberry.*

William and Rebecca
16in (41cm) fully-jointed bears in tan distressed mohair. ***William*** dressed in blue sailor suit. ***Rebecca*** dressed in cotton flower print dress with imported batiste pinafore. Encased in 20in (51cm) wooden trunk.
PRODUCTION: Limited Edition 100
ORIGINAL PRICE: $460.00 each
CURRENT VALUE: $1175.00 each

HODGES, DONNA

P.O. Box 959
La Jolla, California 92038

TRADE NAME: The Bearons of La Jolla

Donna has been making teddy bears since 1985 after selling two family owned educational toy shops in San Diegc, California. She had an extensive sewing and craft background and that enticed her to make her first bears. The materials she uses are of the finest quality, including mohair, alpaca and blends, with ultra suede for paws. Fine quality fabrics are used for the individually designed costumes. Donna enjoys sharing her world of teddy bears with her nine grandchildren.

Lil' Guys and Gals Collection
7in (18cm) alpaca bears. Eight bears in collection wearing a variety of outfits, stand or sit on bases.
PRODUCTION: Limited Edition 100
ORIGINAL PRICE: $230.00 each
CURRENT VALUE: $575.00 each

Goldilocks and The Three Bears
6in (15cm) porcelain ***Goldilocks*** costumed in imported batiste dress and apron. Three bears of alpaca are 7½in (19cm), 6½in (17cm) and 4½in (12cm) size.
PRODUCTION: Limited Edition 50
ORIGINAL PRICE: $325.00
CURRENT VALUE: $800.00

Ashley and Her Wardrobe
15in (38cm) tan mohair bear dressed in lace teddy with necklace. Accessories include nightgown, dress, pinafore, country rag doll and toys, all encased in blue distressed wooden armoire, 22in (56cm).
PRODUCTION: Limited Edition 100
ORIGINAL PRICE: $450.00 set
CURRENT VALUE: $1100.00 set

Father Christmas of Abundance
15in (38cm) bear in tan distressed mohair. First in the Old World Father Christmas series. Dressed in tapestry vest, suede cloth breeches, topped with wide collared full length coat.
PRODUCTION: Limited Edition 25
ORIGINAL PRICE: $450.00
CURRENT VALUE: $1075.00

Jessica
15in (38cm) fully-jointed bear in tan alpaca dressed in white batiste christening dress with slip and panties. She sits in replica carriage lined in batiste, lace and ribbons.
PRODUCTION: Limited Edition 25
ORIGINAL PRICE: $450.00
CURRENT VALUE: $1075.00

HOWEY, SHIRLEY

2064 E. Birchwood
Mesa, Arizona 85204
TRADENAME: Shirley Howey Bears

Shirley has been working with miniatures for many years, but she actually learned how to make teddy bears form her husband Roy. They are both noted bear makers, with Shirley specializing in miniatures. Shirley was a professional quilter at one time, and this talent has certainly aided her in her work with tiny teddies. She and Roy have five children and fourteen grandchildren.

Sadly, Roy Howey passed away and will be missed by all who knew and loved him.

Adam
5in (13cm) teddy in mohair, fully jointed. Cloisonne logo pendant.
INTRODUCED: 1988
PRODUCTION: 15
ORIGINAL PRICE: $50.00
CURRENT VALUE: $125.00

Holly-Beary
3in (8cm) fully-jointed teddies in miniature mohair. Holly is green with red lace collar, Beary is red with green lace collar.
INTRODUCED: 1988
PRODUCTION: One-of-a-kind
ORIGINAL PRICE: $45.00 each
CURRENT VALUE: $125.00 each

Seth
3½in (9cm) fully-jointed bear in mohair. Variety of colors.
INTRODUCED: 1988
ORIGINAL PRICE: $40.00
CURRENT VALUE: $100.00

Bingo
2in (5cm) mohair bear on cast metal wheels.
INTRODUCED: 1984
PRODUCTION: Limited Edition 50
ORIGINAL PRICE: $68.00
CURRENT VALUE: $300.00

HUGHES, ELVA

P.O. Box 192
Hinsdale, Massachusetts 01235
TRADE NAME: Barrington Bears

Elva began bear making in 1978 with a pattern purchased at a store. Her talents quickly developed in creating her own designs, and she finds it a challenge to follow through with a new idea. Elva enjoys making bears with a funny theme and to watch the smiles of adults and the giggles of children. She recently returned to bear making after a year's absence due to nerve damage in her hands. She has many ideas to work with, but must get back into bear making gradually.

Boomer
10in (25cm) fully-jointed bear in gold mohair.
INTRODUCED: 1985
PRODUCTION: Limited Edition 10
ORIGINAL PRICE: $90.00
CURRENT VALUE: $325.00

Rain Bear
Gold mohair bear with swivel head, leather harness and bells. Removable antlers.
INTRODUCED: 1986
ORIGINAL PRICE: $68.00
CURRENT VALUE: $225.00

Halloween Series
9in (23cm) mohair bears, each with costume and mask. Group included frog, clown, mouse, duck, pig and Miss Piggy.
INTRODUCED: 1986
PRODUCTION: Limited Edition 10 each style
ORIGINAL PRICE: $68.00 each
CURRENT VALUE: $225.00 each

Ladybears
11in (28cm) fully-jointed bear produced in both mohair and synthetic. Wears lace skirt with pink ribbon.
INTRODUCED: 1983
PRODUCTION: 200
ORIGINAL PRICE: $65.00 (synthetic); $125.00 (mohair)
CURRENT VALUE: $250.00 (synthetic); $525.00 (mohair)

INMAN, ANN

Rt. 3, Box 161
Hayden, ID 83835
TRADE NAME: Annemade

Ann started in the early 1980s by making a bear at a local craft store. Starting with a simple pattern, she gradually developed her own line of artist bears. Today her line includes a wide variety of bears, including a mechanical bear. Life at Ann's home is never dull, with a family of five children to raise and bear orders to fill.

Hunny Bears
Fully-jointed mohair bears made in 12in (31cm) and 20in (51cm) size.
INTRODUCED: 1988
PRODUCTION: 15 pieces (12in); 20 pieces (20in)
ORIGINAL PRICE: $129.99 (12in); $195.00 (20in)
CURRENT VALUE: $300.00 (12in); $475.00 (20in)

Nicholas and Baby Boo
26in (66cm) mohair bear with steel frame mechanism. Animated bear hugs and kisses Baby Boo while gently waving his lighted candle.
INTRODUCED: 1987
PRODUCTION: 20
ORIGINAL PRICE: $595.00
CURRENT VALUE: $1675.00

KATZOPOULOS, LINDA

225 W. King St.
Hillsborough, North Carolina 27278
TRADE NAME: Linda's Bear-iety Bears

Linda presently lives in North Carolina, where she was born and raised. She has also lived in California and Pennsylvania. Her bear making began in 1985, and her first show was Linda Mullins famous show in San Diego, California. At first she called her bears "Linda's Bears," but it became apparent that there were other artists named Linda, so she changed it to **Linda's Bear-iety Bears,** the name she is currently using.

Abigail Alicia
27in (69cm) fully-jointed bunny in long white synthetic plush, pellet filled.
PRODUCTION: 10
ORIGINAL PRICE: $250.00
CURRENT VALUE: $500.00

Three Angels
Two angels (***Michael*** and ***Daniel***) are 12in (31cm), fully-jointed, made in gold distressed and white mohair. Littlest angel is 4½in (12cm) in gold mohair. All hand stitched.
PRODUCTION: 10
ORIGINAL PRICE: $185.00 (12in); $150.00 (4½in)
CURRENT VALUE: $400.00 (12in); $325.00 (4½in)

Clarence
17in (43cm) fully-jointed bear in synthetic fur. Blue and white tapestry bow.
INTRODUCED: 1988
PRODUCTION: One-of-a-kind
ORIGINAL PRICE: $50.00
CURRENT VALUE: $100.00

KING, BARBARA

1553 Ridgeway Dr.
Glendale, California 91202
TRADE NAME: Barbara King Bears

Like many of today's outstanding artists, Barbara got her start by attending a class in 1987 on how to make a jointed teddy bear. She says that her life has not been the same since that day. Barbara is not new to sewing, having spent many years sewing for herself, children and grandchildren. She also did years of quilting and crafts. Now her time is spent creating new teddy designs.

Emily
21in (53cm) fully-jointed teddy made from child's antique coat. Outfitted in antique dress. Stuffed with excelsior.
PRODUCTION: One-of-a-kind
ORIGINAL PRICE: $300.00
CURRENT VALUE: $700.00

KING, DORIS
4353 Landolt Ave.
Sacramento, California 95821
TRADE NAME: Doris King Originals
Doris spent years making clothing for her children, tailoring clothing for adults, and designing and making outfits for dolls. She made her first teddy bear in 1983, showed it to a friend who owned a shop, and after filling orders for her, she has been producing bears ever since. Doris is appreciative of the bear business, as it has given her the opportunity to design and create. She is also pleased with the many great people she has met at shows and conventions, and grateful for the way her bears are accepted. Doris has six children and 18 grandchildren. *Photograph by Bob Allen.*

KOCH, BARBARA J.
6901 W. North Ln.
Peoria, Arizona 85345
TRADE NAME: B.J.'s Bears & My Honey's Woods
Barbara attended her first bear show in 1984 and was overwhelmed with the bears and artists but after talking with several artists she was encouraged to try her first bear. She started with commercial patterns and 1988 created her own design. Today she produces teddies from 3in (8cm) to 24in (61cm). Barbara has three children (including an 11 year old who has started making bears) and a husband who creates furniture for her bears.

Cassie
Barbara's first design, a 13in (33cm) fully-jointed bear in golden honey mohair. Elbows and knees are also jointed. Lace collar.

INTRODUCED: 1988
PRODUCTION: Limited Edition 50
ORIGINAL PRICE: $82.00
CURRENT VALUE: $175.00

Jeffrey
14in (36cm) fully-jointed bear in German acrylic blue bow on neck.
PRODUCTION: 300
ORIGINAL PRICE: $65.00
CURRENT VALUE: $150.00

KRANTZ, JENNY

810 Division St.
Owosso, Michigan 48867
TRADE NAME: Owassa Bear Co.

Jenny is one of many teddy bear artist/collectors who came to us from the world of dolls. Since teddies seem to be a great companion for dolls, they frequently end up in doll collections, and in Jenny's case, teddy bears were not satisfied to share her attention, they demanded it all, and her collection changed in direction to focus entirely on bears. She then discovered the wonderful world of making bears, designing bears and enjoying the excitement and challenge of being in the bear business full time. Jenny is married to Richard Krantz, who frequently accompanies her to shows and conventions. They have three children and 11 grandchildren.

T-Kayo
14in (36cm) fully-jointed bear produced in mohair. Boxing gloves and shorts.
PRODUCTION: 25
ORIGINAL PRICE: $90.00
CURRENT VALUE: $225.00

Chetta
14in (36cm) fully-jointed teddy in acrylic, blue bow on neck with flower in ear.
PRODUCTION: 500
ORIGINAL PRICE: $55.00
CURRENT VALUE: $125.00

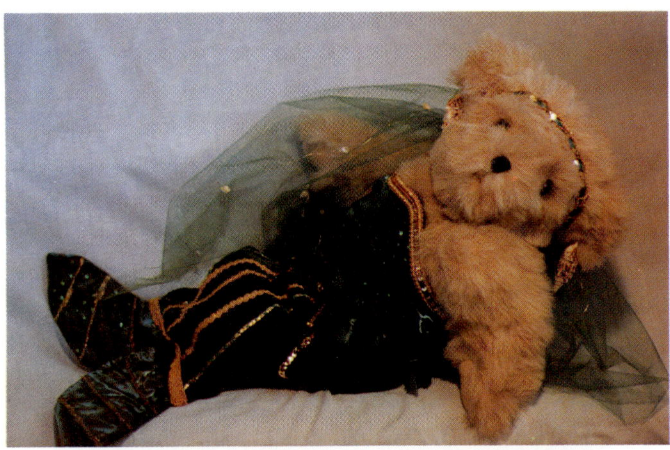

Mermaid
15in (38cm) teddy costumed as mermaid. Tan or off-white fur. Removable costume of velvet and satin.
INTRODUCED: 1988
PRODUCTION: Limited Edition 25
ORIGINAL PRICE: $75.00
CURRENT VALUE: $175.00

KYNION, ANN

P.O. Box 3882
Springfield, Missouri 65808

TRADE NAME: Beana Bears, Etc.

Ann Kynion, a native Missourian, has spent most of her adulthood in the Ozarks. She and her husband Clark have three children. Creating one-of-a-kind bears is Ann's most rewarding aspect of the bear business. She also enjoys meeting people who collect her bears. She and her work have appeared in print media and television. *Photographs by Ann Kynion.*

Posey
14in (36cm) fully-jointed teddy produced in off-white mohair. Pellet stuffed.
PRODUCTION: Limited Edition 100
ORIGINAL PRICE: $85.00
CURRENT VALUE: $175.00

Blackbeary
12in (31cm) fully-jointed bear produced in black mohair with white muzzle. Honey pot hand thrown by Texas potter Jack Hooker.
PRODUCTION: Limited Edition 25
ORIGINAL PRICE: $82.00
CURRENT VALUE: $175.00

Madame Bearina
Soft, poseable plush ballerina whose paws are tied together so she can hang on a doorknob or fit around a child's neck to be danced with.
PRODUCTION: 50
ORIGINAL PRICE: $63.00
CURRENT VALUE: $125.00

Theodore
12in (31cm) fully-jointed teddy in distressed mohair. Growler.
PRODUCTION: Limited Edition 25
ORIGINAL PRICE: $76.00
CURRENT VALUE: $175.00

LANDSTRA, BEV MILLER

87505 Biggs Rd.
Veneta, Oregon 97487

TRADE NAME: Bev Landstra Collectables

Bev says she feels like a veteran in the world of teddy bears, having designed her own patterns since April of 1963 and having started her full-time bear business in January of 1983. Being a meticulous artist, Bev uses only the finest materials available and does all of the design work as well as making the entire bear. She has won her share of awards through the years, but she feels her biggest reward are her customers, and she has them to thank for her success.

T.R. Bear
12½in (32cm) bear in acrylic plush, jointed arms and legs. Paws and pads, muzzle, inside of ear made of camel hair. Mohair eyebrows and mustache, nose made of marble X.
INTRODUCED: 1987
PRODUCTION: Limited Edition 150
ORIGINAL PRICE: $350.00
CURRENT VALUE: $900.00

Theodora and Barney
Largest bear of this pair is 9½in (24cm) fully-jointed, in beige mohair. Muzzle, inside of ear, paws and pads of camel hair. Nose of marble X. Acrylic eyes are covered with camel hair. Mohair eye lashes. ***Barney bear*** is 3½in (9cm), fully-jointed, cream mohair.
INTRODUCED: 1987
PRODUCTION: Limited Edition 75
ORIGINAL PRICE: $175.00 set
CURRENT VALUE: $450.00 set

Moet
8in (20cm) fully-jointed bear in champagne color distressed mohair. Leather paw pads. Fairy costume with wings, halo and wand.
INTRODUCED: 1988
PRODUCTION: 15
ORIGINAL PRICE: $70.00
CURRENT VALUE: $175.00

Ling Ling Panda
8in (20cm) fully-jointed bear produced in black and white mohair. Amber glass eyes, leather paw pads.
INTRODUCED: 1988
PRODUCTION: 10
ORIGINAL PRICE: $85.00
CURRENT VALUE: $200.00

LAPOINTE, SHARON

1782 Tracy Ln.
Auburn, California 95603

Sharon has always loved teddy bears, but it was not until 1982 that she made her first jointed bear. Soon after she began to design her own patterns. Her father's first teddy was the inspiration for Sharon's first design. The bear has been played with by three generations of children, and now resides at Sharon's house, overseeing her work. *Photograph by J.C. Penney Company.*

Susie, Timmy, Toby
All 13in (33cm) in size, fully jointed. ***Susie*** is made in synthetic plush, ***Timmy*** and ***Toby*** are made in imported plush.
INTRODUCED: 1988
PRODUCTION: 25
ORIGINAL PRICE: $120.00 (***Susie***); $135.00 (***Timmy, Toby***)
CURRENT VALUE: $275.00 (***Susie***); $300.00 (***Timmy, Toby***)

LAVERTY, LOIS

206 Riverneck Rd.
Chelmsford, Massachusetts 01824
TRADE NAME: Gile Teddy Bears
Prior to entering the world of teddy bear design in the mid 1980s, Lois had a good deal of experience in dress making and tailoring. She now spends full time at her teddy bear designing and making, doing all the work herself and using only the best materials available. Her greatest reward is seeing each design come to life, and the happiness it brings to people of all ages.

Crystal
23in (58cm) fully-jointed bear in white plush fur. Short fur paws and foot pads.
INTRODUCED: 1985
PRODUCTION: 50
ORIGINAL PRICE: $135.00
CURRENT VALUE: $425.00

Miss Mugsy
14in (36cm) fully-jointed bear in pink plush. Also made in other sizes.
INTRODUCED: 1987
PRODUCTION: 60 (various sizes)
ORIGINAL PRICE: $135.00
CURRENT VALUE: $350.00

LECRONE, MARY KAY
RR #2, Box 125
West Union, Illinois 62477
TRADE NAME: LeBear's

Mary comes from a large creative family and has always been involved in arts and crafts of all forms. Her love for bears began with a teddy bear birthday gift from her husband in 1981. Mary researched information on making bears, and designed her own pattern. They were warmly greeted, and she has been busy ever since filling orders.

Jinx
Fully-jointed bear 6in (15cm) tall in dark tan plush. Comes with fishing pole, hat and stringer of fish.
PRODUCTION: Limited Edition 50
ORIGINAL PRICE: $48.00
CURRENT VALUE: $100.00

Trooper Max
10in (25cm) fully-jointed bear in honey color plush. Wears trooper hat, badge, necktie and service belt with handcuffs and weapon.
PRODUCTION: Limited Edition 250
ORIGINAL PRICE: $120.00
CURRENT VALUE: $225.00

Mitzi
6in (15cm) fully-jointed bear in white plush. Hand crocheted bikini, blanket. Matching bikini, blanket and sun glasses in selection of colors.

PRODUCTION: Limited Edition 100
ORIGINAL PRICE: $48.00
CURRENT VALUE: $100.00

Monty
6in (15cm) fully-jointed bear in tan plush. Handcrafted stick pony.
PRODUCTION: Limited Edition 25
ORIGINAL PRICE: $48.00
CURRENT VALUE: $100.00

Goody Bear
10in (25cm) fully-jointed bear in hand-dyed mohair. Also produced in Bavarian dressed series.
INTRODUCED: 1986
PRODUCTION: Open Edition
ORIGINAL PRICE: $82.00
CURRENT VALUE: $250.00

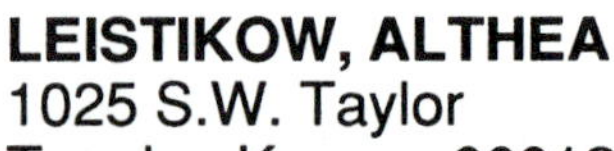

LEISTIKOW, ALTHEA

1025 S.W. Taylor
Topeka, Kansas 66612
TRADE NAME: Bears by Althea

In addition to designing and producing her original bears, Althea also enjoys hunting for and using vintage fabrics in her work. She also makes use of fabrics and accessories from her family collection. Her bears range in size from 5in (13cm) to 32in (81cm). Her design work began in 1984, and in addition to attending various shows and conventions, she also does workshops and lectures on bear making. Her award winning work has been featured in books, magazines, greeting cards and calendars.

Scruff
19in (48cm) fully-jointed bear produced in German synthetic.
PRODUCTION: 26 (Currently produced in different fabric.)
ORIGINAL PRICE: $175.00
CURRENT VALUE: $400.00

LOCKWOOD, WENDY

2644 Knabe Ct.
Carmichael, California 95608
TRADE NAME: Country & Bears

With a degree in Textiles and Business, Wendy is making great use of her educational background in her teddy bear business. She has been designing and making teddy bears since 1984. She does much of the work on the bears, and her husband helps with stuffing and takes care of the paperwork associated with their business. They both enjoy attending shows and meeting the wonderful collectors. They recently have been joined by a new baby daughter, Meghan.

Buttercream
Produced in 20in (51cm) and 23in (58cm) sizes, this fully-jointed bear was produced in 1in (3cm) long buttery cream color mohair.
INTRODUCED: 1987
PRODUCTION: 18
ORIGINAL PRICE: $200.00 (20in); $225.00 (23in)
CURRENT VALUE: $550.00 (20in); $600.00 (23in)

Little Puff
10in (25cm) fully-jointed bear in imported synthetic plush.
PRODUCTION: 20
ORIGINAL PRICE: $60.00
CURRENT VALUE: $150.00

LOW, DONNA

13405 Country Ridge Dr.
Germantown, Maryland 20874
TRADE NAME: Pandas Plus

Donna has been a bear collector for nearly fifteen years, first concentrating on Steiff bears, and then adding artist made teddies. She decided in the mid 1980s to design her own bear, and readily admits that her first one was a total disaster. She says it was so bad that she could not go near her sewing machine for six months. She finally tried again, with better results. Donna changed her pattern many times before she finally achieved the look she was after. Now her biggest problem is being willing to part with a bear when she finishes it.

Buttercup
Fully-jointed 16in (41cm) bear in imported synthetic plush. Individual ultra suede toes and paw pads. Music box.
PRODUCTION: Open edition
ORIGINAL PRICE: $80.00
CURRENT VALUE: $175.00

McCLELLAN, SARAH

8622 E. Oak St.
Scottsdale, Arizona 85257
TRADE NAME: Sal's Pals

Sarah was born in El Paso, Texas and grew up in Minnesota and California. She and her husband and two sons now live in Arizona. She has been producing teddy bears (and dogs, rabbits, horses and dolls) since 1980. Along with teddy bears, Sarah thoroughly enjoys photography and bicycling.

Toothy Teddy
19in (48cm) fully-jointed teddy produced in shaggy plush. This unusual bear has a hand sculpted mouth, nose and claws. Dressed version was sold as "Squire Toothy Teddy." Note: both bears are now produced in European plush under the name Toothy Teddy II and Squire Toothy Teddy II.
PRODUCTION: Limited Edition 100
ORIGINAL PRICE: $250.00
CURRENT VALUE: $750.00

Michelle and Edward's Recital
16in (41cm) fully-jointed teddy bears produced in tan mohair. Black velvet outfits, patent leather shoes. Reugge musical movement. Wooden violin.
INTRODUCED: 1988
PRODUCTION: Limited Edition 50 each
ORIGINAL PRICE: $345.00 each
CURRENT VALUE: $925.00 each

McCONNELL, BARBARA

944 W. Ninth Ave.
Escondido, California 92025
TRADE NAME: McB Bears

Barbara started McB Bears in 1986 after attending her first teddy bear show. She had taken some of the bears she designed to the show, and they sold out quickly. Barbara's business has grown dramatically in the relatively short time she has been in business. She travels extensively throughout the country to sign her bears in the shops that handle them. They are also sold in six other countries. Barbara lives with her husband Keven and two children in a 90 year old home in Escondido, California. *Photograph by Barbara McConnell.*

McELWAIN, MAUREEN COVERT

3209 Marie Dr.
Raleigh, North Carolina 27604
TRADE NAME: Marsh Creek Bears

Maureen has some experience making stuffed toys for her children when they were small, but it was not until 1985 that she discovered bears with a pattern suggested by a friend. She quickly realized that commercial patterns were limiting her creative talent and ideas, so she began to design her own. Her current designs range from 3in (8cm) to over 30in (76cm) and are produced in a variety of fabrics, with mohair being her favorite.

Sarah and Christopher
8in (20cm) fully-jointed bear in mohair. ***Christopher*** wears hand-knit sweater. Produced in a variety of outfits.
PRODUCTION: 100
ORIGINAL PRICE (*Sarah*): $50.00
CURRENT VALUE: $125.00
ORIGINAL PRICE (*Christopher*): $60.00
CURRENT VALUE: $150.00

Izaac Walton
12in (31cm) fully-jointed teddy produced in mohair with hand-knit sweater. Leather paw pads.
PRODUCTION: 10
ORIGINAL PRICE: $65.00
CURRENT VALUE: $150.00

Charlotte
This 27in (69cm) fully-jointed bear was made in domestic synthetic. She has leather paw pads and wears a size three child's dress. All dressed differently.
PRODUCTION: 10
ORIGINAL PRICE: $200.00
CURRENT VALUE: $475.00

Bare Baby
Produced in domestic synthetic in variety of colors. Jointed legs, floppy arms attached at neck. Safety eyes. Trimmed with lace and ribbon. This was artist's first original pattern.
PRODUCTION: 285
ORIGINAL PRICE: $25.00
CURRENT VALUE: $75.00

MALCOLM, MELODIE

73698 CSAH 15
Dassel, Minnesota 55325

TRADE NAME: Fancy Stuffins

Melodie grew up in Florida and now lives in the Minnesota countryside in a 100 year old farmhouse. She has a varied work background, including flight attendant, secretary, radio dispatcher, real estate loan processor, licensed practical nurse and doll maker. While living and working in various national parks in California and Minnesota, Melodie had many real bear related experiences. Her interest in bears led her to create teddies, which she started in the early 1980s.

Rosemary
15in (38cm) fully-jointed teddy in sand color mohair. Wears a rose heart-print country dress with 22 count Victorian floral design cross stitched collar.
INTRODUCED: 1988
PRODUCTION: Limited Edition 20
ORIGINAL PRICE: $200.00
CURRENT VALUE: $475.00

Grandma Henny
19in (48cm) bear in distressed mohair. Fully jointed. Mechanical. Head rotates while music box plays. Wears handmade glasses and crocheted collar.
INTRODUCED: 1988
PRODUCTION: Limited Edition 100
ORIGINAL PRICE: $240.00
CURRENT VALUE: $575.00

Pandora
9in (23cm) teddy in silver gray mohair. Fully jointed. Wears bow on head and carries miniature patchwork quilt.
INTRODUCED: 1988
PRODUCTION: Limited Edition 100
ORIGINAL PRICE: $100.00
CURRENT VALUE: $250.00

Sebastian
10in (25cm) fully-jointed bear produced in silver gray/black tipped mohair. Wears a bib tuxedo.
INTRODUCED: 1988
PRODUCTION: Limited Edition 100
ORIGINAL PRICE: $100.00
CURRENT VALUE: $250.00

Webster
10in (25cm) fully-jointed teddy produced in brown tipped mohair. Imitation leather paws.
INTRODUCED: 1988
PRODUCTION: Limited Edition 100
ORIGINAL PRICE: $90.00
CURRENT VALUE: $225.00

The Twins (Wendy and Willie)
15in (38cm) fully-jointed teddies in acrylic plush. Unique foot and paw pads of solid oak or walnut. Polyester cotton outfits.
PRODUCTION: 29
ORIGINAL PRICE: $130.00 a pair
CURRENT VALUE: $300.00 a pair

MANNON, BECKY

211 W. Third
Kimball, Nebraska 69145

Becky has always been creative in making doll clothes as a child, and producing handcrafted gifts for friends and family. Her husband Steve encouraged her to market her creative work, so she began with an original doll. She soon discovered teddy bears, and this has been her greatest venture. She has recently added a miniature bear to her line. *Photograph by Loring Photography.*

MARTIN, CAROL AND HENRY

515 N. Fourth St.
Arkansas City, Kansas 67005
TRADE NAME: cm Bears

Carol has always enjoyed teddy bears, and still has her first bear, a 1950 Knickerbocker. It was not until 1984 that she made her first bear, and now both she and Henry are kept busy, Carol in making bears and Henry in making accessories and keeping up with the paper work. cm Bears are designed with hand sculptured center seam heads, and all wear a brass name plate which lists the bear's name and edition number (if limited). Carol and Henry are both in the education profession, and when they are not teaching or making bears, they thoroughly enjoy traveling to bear shows and meeting others who enjoy bears. The Martins' have two sons, Chadwick and Detrick. *Photographs by Chadwick Martin.*

Mr. French
16in (41cm) fully-jointed bear in tipped mohair, leather pads. Wears white collar with gray necktie.
INTRODUCED: 1987
PRODUCTION: Limited Edition 67
ORIGINAL PRICE: $88.00
CURRENT VALUE: $250.00

Bare Bear
10in (25cm) fully-jointed bear in tan mohair with leather pads. Carol's first mohair design.
INTRODUCED: 1987
PRODUCTION: Limited Edition 500
ORIGINAL PRICE: $59.00
CURRENT VALUE: $150.00

Opal
Fully-jointed 12in (31cm) bear produced in plum color mohair. A knitting bear sitting on upholstered hassock.
INTRODUCED: 1988
PRODUCTION: Limited Edition 67
ORIGINAL PRICE: $98.00
CURRENT VALUE: $250.00

Aunt Nan
8in (20cm) fully-jointed bear in brown wavy mohair. Comes with easel and "self portrait."
INTRODUCED: 1988
PRODUCTION: Limited Edition 46
ORIGINAL PRICE: $78.00
CURRENT VALUE: $200.00

Carol Ann
11in (28cm) gold distressed mohair bear, fully jointed. Comes with 4in (10cm) unjointed teddy. Produced exclusively for Suzanne DePee.
INTRODUCED: 1988
PRODUCTION: Limited Edition 43
ORIGINAL PRICE: $80.00
CURRENT VALUE: $200.00

Grover
10in (25cm) bear in cinnamon mohair with leather pads. Fully jointed. Bear comes with crocheted rag rug and miniature catalogue. Produced exclusively for Groves Quality Collectibles.
INTRODUCED: 1988
PRODUCTION: Limited Edition 33
ORIGINAL PRICE: $80.00
CURRENT VALUE: $200.00

Bonnie
13in (33cm) fully-jointed bear in antique gold mohair. Comes with a stick horse in chocolate brown mohair.
INTRODUCED: 1988
PRODUCTION: Limited Edition 30
ORIGINAL PRICE: $89.00
CURRENT VALUE: $225.00

Casey Jones
24in (61cm) fully-jointed bear in synthetic plush.
PRODUCTION: 2
ORIGINAL PRICE: $175.00
CURRENT VALUE: $375.00

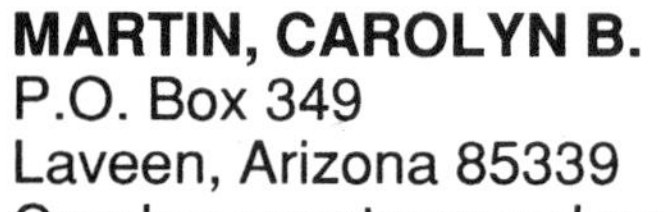

MARTIN, CAROLYN B.

P.O. Box 349
Laveen, Arizona 85339

Carolyn spent several years working with handcrafted dolls before making her first bear from a commercial pattern. She loved making bears, and decided to create her own originals. After three years of doing her own designs, she began to work with leather and fur and decided it was a natural combination. This gave birth to her leather face designs. She sometimes feels it is hard to give them up once she has completed a bear. *Photograph by Carolyn Martin.*

Leather Face Cubs
Fully-jointed cub bears. Rust and gray cubs are mohair, brown cub is in synthetic plush. All have full leather faces, leather eyelids and noses. Cubs were produced in many furs and colors.
PRODUCTION: Open Edition
ORIGINAL PRICE: $95.00 (synthetic); $120.00 (mohair)
CURRENT VALUE: $200.00 (synthetic); $250.00 (mohair)

MARTIN, CINDY

5720 E. Kaviland
Fresno, California 93727
TRADE NAME: Yesterbears

Cindy designed her first bear in 1982, a small button-jointed bear for her daughters. Today she has well over 38 different designs in her line, ranging in size from 3¼in (8cm) up to 54in (137cm). Cindy is always most pleased to hear that someone has gotten pleasure from one of her creations. Cindy lives in California with her husband Gary and their two daughters Wendy and Cory. *Photographs by Cindy and Gary Martin.*

Yesterbear
21in (53cm) fully-jointed teddy in short nap mohair with suede paws.
INTRODUCED: 1985
PRODUCTION: Open Edition
ORIGINAL PRICE: $300.00
CURRENT VALUE: $1025.00

Morris
25in (64cm) mohair bear, fully jointed.
INTRODUCED: 1987
PRODUCTION: 30
ORIGINAL PRICE: $450.00
CURRENT VALUE: $1225.00

Jester
8in (20cm) fully-jointed bear produced in white and antique maroon mohair, light gold mohair paws and head. Ultra suede hat and neck piece.
INTRODUCED: 1987
PRODUCTION: Open Edition
ORIGINAL PRICE: $300.00
CURRENT VALUE: $850.00

Languid Longfellow
15in (38cm) fully-jointed teddy produced in imported rayon fabric. Bends at elbows and knees for poseability.
INTRODUCED: 1987
PRODUCTION: Open Edition
ORIGINAL PRICE: $200.00
CURRENT VALUE: $550.00

Zucchini
14in (36cm) fully-jointed bear in two-toned mohair.
INTRODUCED: 1987
PRODUCTION: Open Edition
ORIGINAL PRICE: $350.00
CURRENT VALUE: $1000.00

Monsieur Goo Bear
12in (31cm) teddy bear in cinnamon/rust cotton stretch velour. Foot pads of vintage deer leather. Jointed arms and legs. White cotton chef cap. Bear carried a wire whisk or wooden spoon.
INTRODUCED: 1983
PRODUCTION: 9
ORIGINAL PRICE: $80.00
CURRENT VALUE: $325.00

MASOR, SHER

469 Crandall Dr.
Worthington, Ohio 43085

TRADE NAME: The Wicker Buggy

Before realizing that the best use of her creative talents was making teddy bears for a living, Sher had numerous jobs, including telephone installer, school bus driver, figure model for graduate art students, belly dancer and instructor. She had been making cloth dolls, toys and a few teddies since 1976, adding miniature hand stitched felt teddies in 1979. By 1982 when she moved to Colorado, she was established in the bear business. Sher describes her designs as being serious whimsy.

Ashley Bluebearrie
14in (36cm) fully-jointed bear in acrylic plush. She wears handmade wings and is costumed in tulle and dazzle fabrics.
PRODUCTION: Limited Edition 50
ORIGINAL PRICE: $100.00
CURRENT VALUE: $225.00

Cream Cheese
15in (38cm) fully-jointed bear produced in ivory shearling. She wears a cotton print dress and patched apron.
PRODUCTION: Limited Edition 50
ORIGINAL PRICE: $110.00
CURRENT VALUE: $250.00

MASTERSON, KARINE

435 Montebello
Ventura, California 93004

TRADE NAME: Karine's

Karine left her career as a costume designer a few years ago and entered the exciting world of the teddy bear artist. One of her greatest pleasures in her newly chosen field is the opportunity to work at home with her little daughter, Sara, who helps with packing. She is also pleased to be able to spend more time with her husband, Rick. Karine says she does not miss her work as a costume designer because she now uses that talent in designing clothes for her bears. All of her designs include costuming.

MEAD, LINDA
P.O. Box 56
Interlochen, Michigan 49643
TRADE NAME: Tea-Bere-Y Hollow Originals
Linda has been creating her line of original designs since 1985. Being a grandmother of three keeps her in touch with the child inside that helps her to create a wide range of styles. She comes from a creative family and learned to sew at an early age. This led to designing doll clothes and later wedding dresses and other adult clothing. This background made it a natural progression to her work with teddy bears. She is assisted by her husband, Gordon.

O'l Gruff
Standing on all fours, this bear measures 36in (91cm) long and 24in (61cm) tall. Constructed with wooden frame to hold weight of an adult. Produced in synthetic plush, shaved face, suede cloth nose. Paw prints on all four feet.
INTRODUCED: 1987
ORIGINAL PRICE: $180.00
CURRENT VALUE: $450.00

Wisteria Wisteria
This 14in (36cm) fully-jointed teddy was originally designed for a contest sponsored by the Teddy Bear Boosters luncheon in California in May of 1988. She won the Member's Choice ribbon. The bear is produced in white alpaca, with the body dyed light green. The bear's shoulders are adorned with silk "wisteria" blossoms.
INTRODUCED: 1988
PRODUCTION: 4
ORIGINAL PRICE: $125.00
CURRENT VALUE: $300.00

MEDIATE, FLORA
190 Malcolm Dr.
Pasadena, California 91105
TRADE NAME: Flora's Teddys
Flora has been an art teacher for many years, and began making toys after the birth of her first child. Her first teddy was created in 1981 at the request of a shop owner, where her designs were being sold. This was the beginning of a very productive avocation for Flora, who has been frequently recognized with first place ribbons for her designs. *Photograph by Flora and Frank Mediate.*

MICHAUD, DORIS AND TERRY

505 W. Broad St.
Chesaning, Michigan 48616
TRADE NAME: Carrousel by Michaud
The Michauds are widely-known throughout the United States and in other countries. They were one of the early pioneers in the modern teddy bear hobby, having collected antique teddies for over twenty years. They designed their first teddy bear in the late 1970s and were encouraged by the late Peter Bull to market them. In addition to marketing their bears around the world, they write, lecture and travel extensively to spread the good word about artist and antique teddy bears. *Photographs by Thomas Mocny.*

Michigan Sesquicentennial Bear
19in (48cm) fully-jointed bear in domestic plush. This bear was commissioned by the Michigan Department of Commerce as the official bear for the Michigan Sesquicentennial in 1987. Two editions of 150 each were produced.
INTRODUCED: 1987
PRODUCTION: Limited Edition 300
ORIGINAL PRICE: $150.00
CURRENT VALUE: $400.00

Uncle Sam
19in (48cm) fully-jointed teddy produced for the anniversary of Theodore Roosevelt. Felt hat and jacket, satin vest, striped trousers of trigger. Brass tag on gold chain with edition number.
INTRODUCED: 1983
PRODUCTION: Limited Edition 200
ORIGINAL PRICE: $150.00
CURRENT VALUE: $650.00

People's Choice
19in (48cm) fully-jointed bear in acrylic plush, produced to commemorate election year. Reversible ribbon carries Democratic and Republican insignia on each side.
INTRODUCED: 1988
PRODUCTION: Open Edition
ORIGINAL PRICE: $96.00
CURRENT VALUE: $225.00

Teddy Snowbird
12in (31cm) fully-jointed bear produced in mohair. Introduced at Walt Disney World's first convention in December 1988.
INTRODUCED: 1988
PRODUCTION: 150
ORIGINAL PRICE: $150.00
CURRENT VALUE: $475.00

The Old Man's Bear
This 19in (48cm) fully-jointed bear in distressed mohair is part of the Michaud's Carrousel Museum Recreation series.
INTRODUCED: 1988
PRODUCTION: Open Edition
ORIGINAL PRICE: $160.00
CURRENT VALUE: $375.00

MILTON, ZELMA

11201 S.W. 55th St. #386
Miramar, Florida 33025

TRADE NAME: Z & J Enterprises

When she produced her first teddy bear in the mid 1980s, Zelma was able to draw on over twenty years of sewing and craft experience. Today she produces teddies as a full-time vocation. She does all of the design work and sewing, including the costumes. Sizes range from 3in (8cm) to 15in (38cm), and she works with European plush or mohair.

Play Time Annie
18in (46cm) fully-jointed bear produced in European plush with blue safety eyes. Wears Sheriff's outfit. Horse not original. Musical movement plays "Home on the Range."
INTRODUCED: 1988
PRODUCTION: Limited Edition 25
ORIGINAL PRICE: $95.00 (with horse)
CURRENT VALUE: $200.00

Daddy's Little Girl
18in (46cm) fully-jointed bride in European plush with brown safety eyes. Dress of bridal lace and satin. Headpiece and bouquet varied with each bear.
INTRODUCED: 1988
PRODUCTION: Limited Edition 25
ORIGINAL PRICE: $150.00
CURRENT VALUE: $350.00

Joanne with Paws for Peace
1990 TOBY® Recipient

MITCHELL, JOANNE

2115 Cypress Landing Rd., Suite #300
Houston, Texas 77090

TRADE NAME: Family Tree Bears

Family Tree Bears started at Joanne's kitchen table in 1984 and has been growing ever since. Joanne's designs have reflected her inherent love of natural woodlands and her strong commitment to preservation. Ranging in size from 6½in (17cm) to over 40in (101cm), each one shares Joanne's pledge of quality, originality of design and attention to every detail. Joanne believes that creativity is a gift from God, and therefore, each bear becomes a silent "thank you" with her signature.

Sam Houston
19in (48cm) fully-jointed bear in synthetic plush. Paw and foot pads in upholstery fabric. Created in honor of Texas Sesquicentennial.
INTRODUCED: 1985
ORIGINAL PRICE: $250.00
CURRENT VALUE: $925.00

Plantation Children
A selection of four different bears, 9in (23cm) tall, fully-jointed, produced in mohair or mohair-alpaca blend. Girl bears each had a rag doll. All bears have lead crystal eyes. Paw and foot pads of pig skin suede.
INTRODUCED: 1988
PRODUCTION: Limited Edition 50 each
ORIGINAL PRICE: $165.00 each
CURRENT VALUE: $425.00 each

Christopher Bearapopolis
15in (38cm) mohair teddy, fully jointed. Part of Immigrant series. Velveteen paw and foot pads.
INTRODUCED: 1988
PRODUCTION: Limited Edition 50
ORIGINAL PRICE: $175.00
CURRENT VALUE: $450.00

Larry
14in (36cm) fully-jointed bear made in long black mohair. Black glass eyes with white at corners. White collar with black bow tie. Signed and dated.
INTRODUCED: 1988
PRODUCTION: Open Edition
ORIGINAL PRICE: $90.00
CURRENT VALUE: $225.00

MORRIS, JACKIE

6977 Tomahawk Trl.
Reynoldsburg, Ohio 43068
TRADE NAME: Blacklick Bears

Jackie was assigned to make a teddy bear when she sat in on her mother's 4-H group at the age of four, and following this first sewing project, she has produced everything from wedding dresses to men's suits. Making teddies to sell at craft shows began in the mid 1980s, producing what she thought were toys for children. She quickly learned that adults collected teddy bears and has since grown to love making bears more than anything she has ever done. *Photograph by Jackie Morris.*

Murphy Bears
Large bear is a 19in (48cm), fully-jointed teddy in vintage synthetic plush. Wears hand-made sweater and antique heart pendant. Smaller bears are 9in (23cm), fully-jointed, produced in vintage tan alpaca fabric. Excelsior stuffed.
INTRODUCED: 1988
PRODUCTION: 5 Large, 15 Small Bears
ORIGINAL PRICE: $185.00 (19in); $60.00 (9in)
CURRENT VALUE: $400.00 (19in); $150.00 (9in)

MURPHY, PAT

6900 Jennings Rd.
Ann Arbor, Michigan 48105
TRADE NAME: Murphy Bears

Pat lives on the outskirts of Ann Arbor, Michigan, where she, her husband and two teen-age daughters share 14 acres with a menagerie of horses, dogs, cats, and of course, many bears. Growing up in a family of antique collectors, Pat has always had a love for antiques, and it has carried over into her bear making. Pat began in 1984 by specializing in vintage fur, but due to the scarcity of old fabrics, she has branched out into using new distressed mohair. Many of her new mohair bears are hand-dyed to create added individuality.

NAGLE, SUSAN WEBBER

15 Laird St.
West Lawn, Pennsylvania 19609
TRADE NAME: Susie's Sewn Originals

Susan began her teddy bear business in the mid 1980s, shortly after graduating from Elizabethtown College with her Bachelor of Science degree in Psychology. She was using her teddy bears in her work as a family therapist working with abused children, but the bears also caught the attention of her co-workers. It was then that Susie's Sewn Originals was born. Susan's grandfather and her father were both in the furrier business, and Susan notes that, like her Taxidermist grandfather, she is still "stuffing bears."

Ashley
14in (36cm) mohair bear, fully jointed. Leather paw pads, hand-knit sweater set.
INTRODUCED: 1988
PRODUCTION: One-of-a-kind
ORIGINAL PRICE: $75.00
CURRENT VALUE: $175.00

Billy Bee Bear
12in (31cm) fully-jointed bear produced in gold mohair. Wears a hat with netting and comes with a beehive covered with bees and honey.
INTRODUCED: 1988
PRODUCTION: Open Edition
ORIGINAL PRICE: $90.00
CURRENT VALUE: $200.00

NEARING, KATHY

38 Montague St.
Binghamton, New York 13901
TRADE NAME: My Kind of Bear

Kathy got into the bear business quite by chance. Several years ago she wanted a teddy bear, but she did not know it was okay for a grandmother to buy a teddy for herself, so she decided to make one. Naturally she could not stop with just one, so making teddies has become a way of life with her.
Photographs by Kathy Nearing.

Charlie
Fully-jointed 14in (36cm) teddy in distressed mohair. Produced in a variety of colors.
INTRODUCED: 1988
ORIGINAL PRICE: $120.00
CURRENT VALUE: $250.00

Peddlar Bear
Sculpted from low temperature German firing compound. Peddler Bear is 1½in (4cm) tall. Bears on tray are ⅜in (.9cm) tall.
INTRODUCED: 1987
PRODUCTION: Limited Edition 300
ORIGINAL PRICE: $38.00
CURRENT VALUE: $100.00

NEAVES, MARY

16 Twin Springs Dr.
Arlington, Texas 76016
TRADE NAME: Mama Bear Creations

Mary is an artisan in the prestigious International Guild of Miniature Artisans, Ltd. Her work can be seen in miniature museums in both Dallas and San Diego. She has combined her love for teddy bears with her talent for designing miniatures and has offered them at shows throughout the United States. She works in 1/12th scale.

NETT, GARY AND MARGARET
601 Taneytown Rd.
Gettysburg, Pennsylvania 17325
TRADE NAME: Bears by Nett
This mother and son team have a well-deserved reputation for the exquisite detail found in their work. Margaret began a professional sewing career nearly 40 years ago, and as a sideline, she produced stuffed animals. The Bears by Nett operation started in 1983 when Gary found himself unemployed. His design experience in architectural construction greatly aided him in designing teddy bears, and he was greatly inspired by his mother, a master at her craft. The quest for perfection in detail is an inherent part of their philosophy. *Photographs by Gary L. Nett.*

Mr. Cinnamon Bear
18in (46cm) teddy bear, fully jointed. Canvas body, head and paws in mohair. This was Netts' first character bear. Comes with book.
INTRODUCED: 1983
PRODUCTION: Limited Edition 240
ORIGINAL PRICE: $150.00
CURRENT VALUE: $675.00

Black Bear
18in (46cm) fully-jointed bear, black alpaca body with tan mohair nose.
INTRODUCED: 1986
PRODUCTION: Open Edition
ORIGINAL PRICE: $150.00
CURRENT VALUE: $500.00

Bear Scout Bear
Fully-jointed 18in (46cm) bear with canvas body, mohair head and paws. Leather shoes. Detailed uniform with authentic replica buttons.
INTRODUCED: 1986
ORIGINAL PRICE: $150.00
CURRENT VALUE: $475.00

Sisters
Fully-jointed bears, 12in (31cm) and 5in (13cm). Larger bear in white mohair, smaller bear in pink or peach mohair.
INTRODUCED: 1987
PRODUCTION: Limited Edition 25 sets
ORIGINAL PRICE: $150.00 set
CURRENT VALUE: $400.00 set

NEWLIN, SUE

519 S. Fifth Ave.
Arcadia, California 91006
TRADE NAME: Sue Newlin Collectibles
Sue is a well-traveled teddy bear artist, having traveled to shows throughout the country and taught a bear making class in Japan in 1988. Her adventures in the world of bear making actually began in 1982. She has kept very busy ever since and recently added dolls to her line. *Photograph by Sue Newlin.*

Grae Waki Bears
Handmade wool felt. Joints are strung with felted buttons. Wool stuffing. All bears identified with woven cloth tag.

Fridgee
23in (58cm)
PRODUCTION: 12
ORIGINAL PRICE: $110.00
CURRENT VALUE: $250.00

Marmalade
12in (31cm)
PRODUCTION: 10
ORIGINAL PRICE: $65.00
CURRENT VALUE: $150.00

Junior Mars
13in (33cm)
PRODUCTION: 14
ORIGINAL PRICE: $75.00
CURRENT VALUE: $175.00

Blue
20in (51cm)
PRODUCTION: 13
ORIGINAL PRICE: $110.00
CURRENT VALUE: $250.00

NICHOLL, DAWN

40 Ross St.
Onerahi-Whangerei
NEW ZEALAND
TRADE NAME: Grae Waki Bears
Dawn is an artist with a unique approach to bear making, living in a unique country. She lives in the north of New Zealand, where the colors and shapes of the country and character of the people influence her bear making. Her bears are handmade, hand-molded felt, produced entirely of New Zealand wool. From the farm the fleece is cleaned and carded, then the hand molding process takes place. Dawn's early bear molds were made of river and beach rocks. Today she utilizes wood, carved to the shapes she wishes the bear to be.

ORLANDO, CAT

70875 Dillon Rd. #26
Desert Hot Springs, California 92240

Cat inherited much of her sewing skills from her talented mother and her grandparents. Although she has been sewing since the age of five, it was not until the encouragement from a friend that her bear making career began in 1986. She has been creating original designs since then, and has inspired her daughter to do the same. Cat frequently travels to shows and thoroughly enjoys meeting new collectors. *Photographs by Ken Yoshitomi.*

My Honey
Fully-jointed 17in (43cm) bear in wavy mohair. Pellet and polyfil stuffed.
INTRODUCED: 1988
PRODUCTION: Limited Edition 200
ORIGINAL PRICE: $149.00
CURRENT VALUE: $350.00

Brandilee
10in (25cm) fully-jointed teddy produced in German synthetic. Pellet and polyfil stuffed. Wears flower wreath and bouquet.
INTRODUCED: 1988
PRODUCTION: Limited Edition 50
ORIGINAL PRICE: $60.00
CURRENT VALUE: $150.00

O'SULLIVAN, JOYCE

4320 196th S.W. #B233
Lynnwood, Washington 98036

TRADE NAME: Need Just A Bear

Need Just A Bear started out as a joint project for Joyce and her mother, Norma, in the mid-1980s. Her mother "cut the apron strings" a few years ago, as Joyce puts it, and she has been producing bears on her own ever since. Joyce designs her patterns from childhood memories or from an inspiration provided by a friend. Ideas come to her all hours of the day so she is constantly taking notes and designing patterns. From the original idea to a completed bear can take up to nine months and several prototypes. Joyce finds this business very rewarding because of the joy it brings others. *Photograph by Patricia Lyons.*

Jason
17in (43cm) fully-jointed teddy produced in beige mohair. Wears satin neck ribbon and gold filigree star.
ORIGINAL PRICE: $150.00
CURRENT VALUE: $325.00

PAUK, CHRISTINA HEMMET

Rt. 1, Box 65
White Oak, North Carolina 28399

TRADE NAME: Bear Works

A former real estate broker for 12 years, Christina started her full-time bear making business in 1987 when she decided to pursue her lifelong dream of designing and creating. She had opportunity to study in Germany and France as a native of Germany and is strongly influenced in her work by her love of antiques and teddy bears. She utilizes fabrics from recycled furs, imported German mohair, and other quality materials. Christina also designs and creates dolls, and on occasion will mix different mediums in her work. She and her husband, John, travel to various shows.

Sailor Boy, Girl
12in (31cm) fully-jointed bears in mohair. Music box in boy.
PRODUCTION: One-of-a-kind
ORIGINAL PRICE: $125.00 (***girl***); $150.00 (***boy***)
CURRENT VALUE: $300.00 (***girl***); $350.00 (***boy***)

Bride Dolly Bear
29in (74cm) fully-jointed, bear face on one side, doll face on reverse. Produced in mohair. Dresses are made from the original bride's dress of the collector.
ORIGINAL PRICE: $525.00
CURRENT VALUE: $1250.00

Patriotic Bear
30in (76cm) fully-jointed bear in imported plush with mohair beard.
PRODUCTION: One-of-a-kind
ORIGINAL PRICE: $350.00
CURRENT VALUE: $825.00

Father Christmas
19in (48cm) fully-jointed bear in mohair. Coat of suede and rabbit.
PRODUCTION: 2
ORIGINAL PRICE: $279.00
CURRENT VALUE: $650.00

Bears on Bike
15in (38cm) fully-jointed bear in mohair.
PRODUCTION: 5
ORIGINAL PRICE; $95.00 (bear only)
CURRENT VALUE: $225.00

PEARCE, CAROL

16126 La Avenida
Houston, Texas 77062
TRADE NAME: Rosebearys
Carol's teddies are identified with a heart on their sleeve. She began collecting bears in 1984 and making bears in 1986. As manager and resident artist of a teddy bear store, Carol is totally involved with teddy bears. *Photographs by Carol Pearce.*

Iva Ellen
16in (41cm) fully-jointed teddy produced in tan alpaca.
INTRODUCED: 1987
PRODUCTION: 9
ORIGINAL PRICE: $150.00
CURRENT VALUE: $375.00

Mary E. Christmas
13½in (34cm) fully-jointed bear in golden tan mohair. Corduroy overalls made by artist's mother, Mary. Red bow in ear, wreath on arm, tangled in battery operated tree lights.
INTRODUCED: 1988
PRODUCTION: Limited Edition 12
ORIGINAL PRICE: $98.00
CURRENT VALUE: $200.00

PHILLIPPI, NEYSA

45 Gorman Ave.
Indiana, Pennsylvania 15701
TRADE NAME: Purely Neysa
When Neysa developed an interest in bears, she had just graduated from the Art Institute of Pittsburgh in 1978. With a toy store located across from her place of employment, Neysa purchased a teddy every pay day. This led to bear designing and making, and in 1985 she became a full-time bear, doll maker and weaver. After her first show in 1989 her doll making and weaving came to an abrupt end, and Neysa devotes all of her creative efforts to her teddy bears.

Draft Bear
24in (61cm) tall, early Draft Bears made of upholstery fabric, later of acrylic plush. Plush fabric head and paws, muslin body. Cotton print dress and bloomers. Most were signed, dated and numbered. Designed to sit against door to keep out draft.
INTRODUCED: 1987
PRODUCTION: 150
ORIGINAL PRICE: $35.00
CURRENT VALUE: $100.00

PHILLIPS, GARY LEE
4889 N. Hermitage
Chicago, Illinois 60640
Gary is very involved in a variety of disciplines, including writing and the fiber arts, such as weaving, spinning and lace making. He also is very involved with designing and producing teddy bears, sharing his Chicago home with several hundred teddy bears.

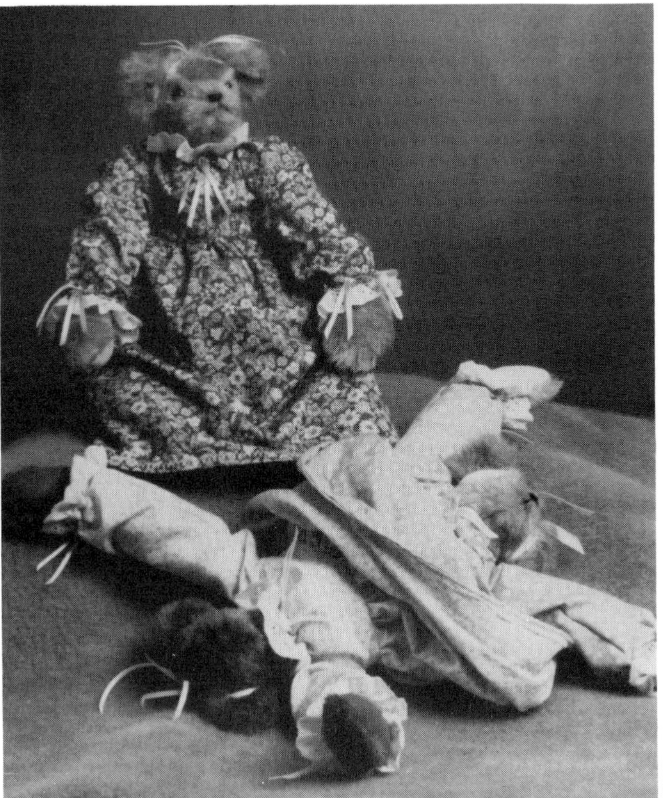

Flip-Flop Bear
11in (28cm) tall. Early Flip-Flop Bears produced in tweed style upholstery fabric, changed to acrylic in 1988. Plush head and paws, muslin body. Safety eyes. Cotton print dresses, which covered second bear.
INTRODUCED: 1987
PRODUCTION: 50
ORIGINAL PRICE: $25.00
CURRENT VALUE: $75.00

Bearistotle
Fully-jointed 12in (31cm) bear in acrylic shag, some brown, some gray. Green or blue eyes. Identified with cloth tag at base of tail.
INTRODUCED: 1988
PRODUCTION: Open Edition
ORIGINAL PRICE: $40.00
CURRENT VALUE: $75.00

Guinevere
12in (31cm) jointed bear in white acrylic plush. Brown safety eyes. Blue or yellow dress. Identified with cloth tag at base of tail.
INTRODUCED: 1988
PRODUCTION: Open Edition
ORIGINAL PRICE: $55.00
CURRENT VALUE: $125.00

Bare Bear
1½in (4cm) fully-jointed with internal joints, hand sewn in velour.
INTRODUCED: 1981
PRODUCTION: Open Edition
ORIGINAL PRICE: $20.00
CURRENT VALUE: $100.00

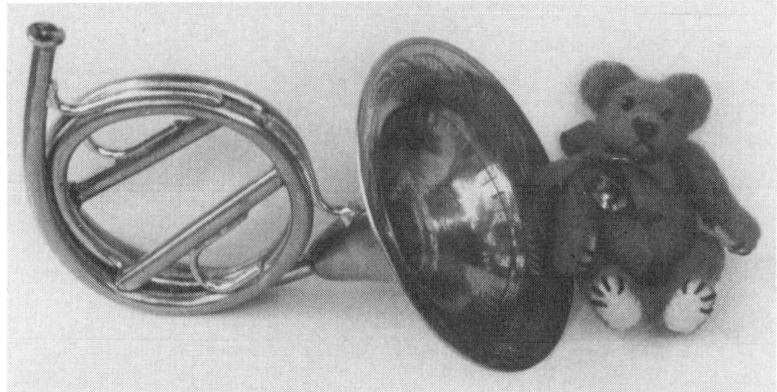

PHILLIPS, SARA

726 Longview Ave.
Westminster, Maryland 21157-5725

Sara has always had interest in miniatures, teddy bears, and making things but she did not start her career as one of the teddy miniature bear makers until 1981. Her work has been recognized with numerous awards, including two Golden Teddy awards and a TOBY® nomination. Since her work is quite elaborate and detailed, her production is very limited. It is even more limited now that she has started a family. *Photographs by Dottie Ayers, Lee Wolf, Bob Repsher.*

Clown Bears
1½in (4cm) fully-jointed with internal joints, hand sewn in velour. Assorted colors.
INTRODUCED: 1981
PRODUCTION: Open Edition
ORIGINAL PRICE: $24.00
CURRENT VALUE: $100.00

Nutcracker Bear
1¼in (3cm) tall. Fully-jointed with internal joints. Open mouth. Came in its own walnut shell home and limited edition tag.
INTRODUCED: 1983
PRODUCTION: Limited Edition 10
ORIGINAL PRICE: $75.00
CURRENT VALUE: $350.00

Jester Bears
Fully-jointed bear with internal joints, 1½in (4cm) high. Hand sewn velour and felt. Variety of colors. A second, more elaborate series introduced in 1984.
INTRODUCED: 1981
PRODUCTION: Open Edition
ORIGINAL PRICE: $27.00
CURRENT VALUE: $125.00

Mini Perfume/Compact
Set is hand sewn, internal joints. 1in (3cm) to 1¼in (3cm). ***Compact Bear*** has removable head with lipstick and compact inside body. ***Perfume Bear*** has removable head, tiny perfume bottle inside body. Assorted colors.
INTRODUCED: 1984
PRODUCTION: Limited Edition 10 sets
ORIGINAL PRICE: $125.00 pair
CURRENT VALUE: $550.00 pair

Open Mouth Panda Clown
1½in (4cm) panda holding ¾in (2cm) hand puppet. Panda fully-jointed with internal joints. Puppet has jointed head.
INTRODUCED: 1986
PRODUCTION: Open Edition
ORIGINAL PRICE: $90.00
CURRENT VALUE: $325.00

POLICKY, ROSE

270 W. Exchange
Astoria, Oregon 97103

Rose's teddy bear career began as a hobby in 1982 while living on a farm in western Nebraska but it did not blossom into a full-time business until her move to Astoria in 1985. Rose works primarily in miniature bears, ranging from a ½in (1cm) up to 9in (23cm) tall. She is pleased that the bear business has given her the opportunity to make some wonderful new friends, and to spend time with her husband and three children.

Astor Longfellow Design by Price and Rose Policky
8in (20cm) tall, jointed arms and legs. Produced in mohair. Also produced in 4in (10cm) and 1⅛in (3cm) sizes.
INTRODUCED: 1988
ORIGINAL PRICE: $68.00
CURRENT VALUE: $150.00

Itty Bitty Buddies
First design by Rose Policky, produced in sizes from 1/2in (1cm) up to 1½in (4cm). Hand sewn ultra suede. Jointed arms and legs.
INTRODUCED: 1985
PRODUCTION: Open Edition
ORIGINAL PRICE: $18.00
CURRENT VALUE: $50.00

Wagger B. Bear
5½in (14cm) bear in mohair, jointed arms and legs.
INTRODUCED: 1986
PRODUCTION: 46
ORIGINAL PRICE: $30.00
CURRENT VALUE: $100.00

QUINN, SUE
Quarriers Village
by Bridge of Weir Renfrewshire
SCOTLAND PA11 3SX
TRADE NAME: Dormouse Designs
Sue began designing toys and teddy bears at the age of 14. She attended the Nottingham School of Art for a time, and after moving to Scotland in 1973, she gradually increased the range of toys she was making. In 1983 she opened premises away from her home, and now Dormouse Designs sell throughout the world. Sue is helped with a small team of people at her workshop, which allows her to concentrate on her range of teddy bears. Sue has written two books on soft toy and teddy bear making, and in 1986 she was awarded the "Toy Maker of the Year" award.

Gryffe Bear
8in (20cm) fully-jointed teddy in woven fur fabric. Produced in five styles; sailor, bear with book, cardigan, cardigan and book, sweater and leather satchel.
INTRODUCED: 1985
PRODUCTION: Limited Edition 25 each style
ORIGINAL PRICE: $40.00
CURRENT VALUE: $150.00

Wee Bairn
14in (36cm) fully-jointed bear in gold mohair. Safety eyes.
INTRODUCED: 1985
PRODUCTION: Limited Edition 100
ORIGINAL PRICE: $40.00
CURRENT VALUE: $150.00

Brambles at Sea
15in (38cm) fully-jointed bear in knitted acrylic plush. Growler. Also produced as ***Brambles Bedtime*** and ***Brambles School Days***.
INTRODUCED: 1986
ORIGINAL PRICE: $50.00
CURRENT VALUE: $150.00

Baby Bracken
15in (38cm) teddy bear in woven plush. Jointed head only. Growler.
INTRODUCED: 1986
ORIGINAL PRICE: $50.00
CURRENT VALUE: $150.00

Dustin
10in (25cm) fully-jointed teddy produced in mohair. Has a ladybug on paw, caterpillar on foot.
INTRODUCED: 1988
PRODUCTION: 12
ORIGINAL PRICE: $95.00
CURRENT VALUE: $225.00

RANKIN, JODI
1007 McCarron Ct.
Gahanna, Ohio 43230
TRADE NAME: Bears By Jodi
Jodi is one of our newer teddy bear artists but a very dedicated bear maker who started as many of us did as a collector, then accepted the challenge to design and make a bear. She and her husband share their home with two children. Jodi was given some assistance in getting started by another Columbus bear maker, Linda Henry. Now she is happily producing her own designs. *Photographs by Carl Rankin.*

Dasie
14in (36cm) fully-jointed bear in wavy mohair.
INTRODUCED: 1988
PRODUCTION: 5
ORIGINAL PRICE: $160.00
CURRENT VALUE: $375.00

REEVES, JANET
640 E. Wheeler Rd.
Midland, Michigan 48640
TRADE NAME: Hug-A-Bear
Hug-A-Bears are found in shops throughout the United States and in Australia. Janet started designing and making her bears in 1985. She says it took several months of research, trial and error, and quite a few laughs before she was able to create what she calls her first satisfactory teddy. Her bears since have won numerous awards and ribbons. *Photographs by Janet Reeves.*

Amanda
12in (31cm) fully-jointed teddy in caramel mohair.
INTRODUCED: 1986
PRODUCTION: Limited Edition 275
ORIGINAL PRICE: $90.00
CURRENT VALUE: $250.00

Whitney
15in (38cm) fully-jointed acrylic plush bear. Velvet paw pads.
INTRODUCED: 1985
ORIGINAL PRICE: $65.00
CURRENT VALUE: $200.00

Duncan
Fully-jointed 10in (25cm) bear in gold mohair and wool blend. Red leather collar with bell.
INTRODUCED: 1988
PRODUCTION: Limited Edition 100
ORIGINAL PRICE: $90.00
CURRENT VALUE: $225.00

Nanuq
17in (43cm) fully-jointed bear in imported synthetic plush. Handmade scarf bearing his name.
INTRODUCED: 1988
PRODUCTION: Limited Edition 75
ORIGINAL PRICE: $175.00
CURRENT VALUE: $425.00

Llda Rose
14in (36cm) fully-jointed bear in light rose color mohair with matching ultra suede paw pads. Lace and ribbon ruff.
INTRODUCED: 1988
PRODUCTION: Limited Edition 500
ORIGINAL PRICE: $130.00
CURRENT VALUE: $300.00

Wessex
18in (46cm) fully-jointed teddy in mohair, with growler. Comes with numbered, signed certificate.
INTRODUCED: 1987
PRODUCTION: Limited Edition 300
ORIGINAL PRICE: $65.00
CURRENT VALUE: $175.00

Huntley
16in (41cm) fully-jointed teddy in fur fabric with safety eyes. Numbered, signed certificate.
INTRODUCED: 1988
PRODUCTION: Limited Edition 200
ORIGINAL PRICE: $55.00
CURRENT VALUE: $125.00

RIXON, SUSAN

51 Dudley Close
Tilehurst
Reading, Berkshire
ENGLAND RG3 6JJ

TRADE NAME: Nonsuch Soft Toys

Susan Rixon started her small company in 1978, and since she was born near the site of King Henry the VIII's Nonsuch Palace, it was the name chosen for her new firm. From small beginnings an exclusive range of teddy bears have been designed and handmade both for children and for collectors worldwide. Her specialty is small limited editions in English fabrics, some of which are produced in colors specifically for her company. She and her husband, David, manage every aspect of their company. They live in Reading with their two sons.

Boscoe
23in (58cm) fully-jointed bear in off-white mohair.
INTRODUCED: 1985
PRODUCTION: Limited Edition 500
ORIGINAL PRICE: $250.00
CURRENT VALUE: $750.00

SCHMIDT, MARIA
536 Sunset Blvd. S.W.
North Canton, Ohio 44720
TRADE NAME: The Charlestowne Bear
Maria (Pronick) Schmidt earned her Bachelor of Fine Arts degree in 1979 and previously worked as a freelance artist begore starting a bear making career in 1983. She is greatly influenced by early German bears. Maria's creations are well thought out and researched before coming to life. Her toys are in limited supply as all work is done by her.
Photographs by Maria Schmidt.

Klein Fritz
18in (46cm) honey mohair bear. Fully jointed.
INTRODUCED: 1986
PRODUCTION: Open Edition
ORIGINAL PRICE: $200.00
CURRENT VALUE: $475.00

Kodi
27in (69cm) fully-jointed bear in honey mohair. Also produced in distressed mohair.
PRODUCTION: Open Edition
ORIGINAL PRICE: $500.00
CURRENT VALUE: $1150.00

SCHUTT, STEVE
201 First Ave. N.W.
Clarion, Iowa 50525
Steve is a multi-talented artist who traces his beginnings in the design and construction of teddy bears to 17 years background in producing puppets. Another talent he is well-known for are original design quilts. Steve started producing teddy bears in 1980, first for the antiques collectors market, for the decorating market, and finally for the artist bear collector market. He has won numerous awards for his work, including two TOBY® nominations, a Golden Teddy award and three Artist Choice awards.

Puppeteer Bear
40in (101cm) fully-jointed bear in mohair. He has eight puppets representing bear versions of characters in Punch and Judy. Artist also produced clown shoes.
ORIGINAL PRICE: $2000.00
CURRENT VALUE: $5100.00

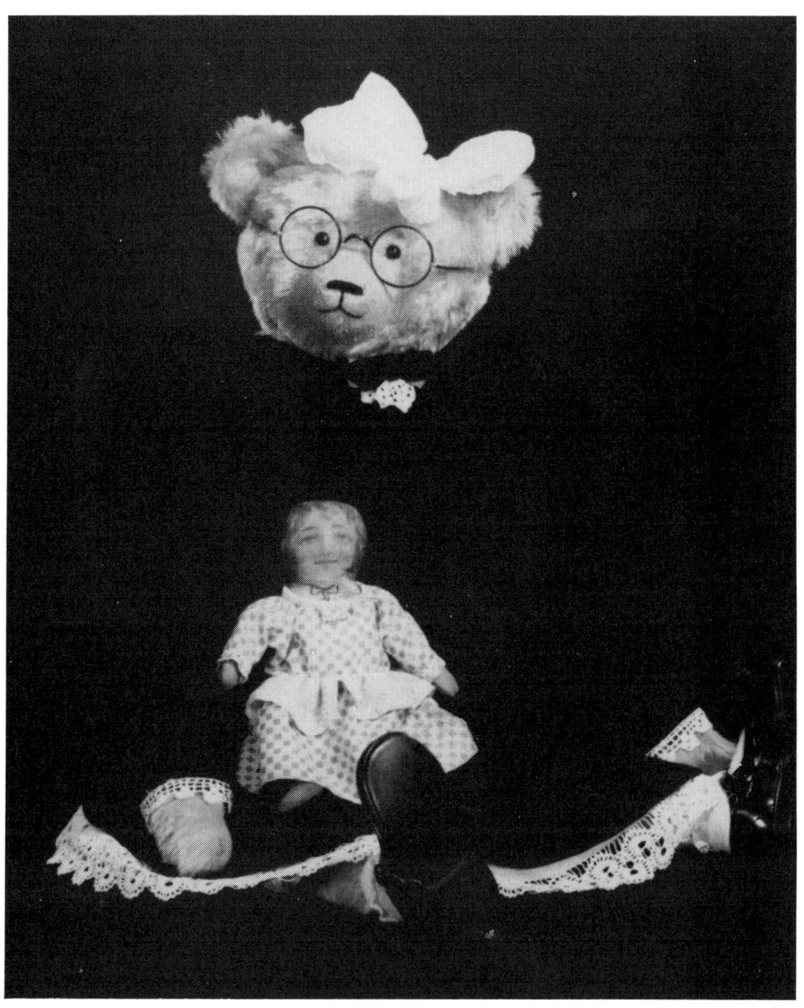

Victoria Anne
34in (86cm) fully-jointed bear in mohair. Wears red velvet dress, shoes.
ORIGINAL PRICE: $1100.00
CURRENT VALUE: $3000.00

Cornelious
26in (66cm) fully-jointed mohair teddy. Wears boots and bandana neck piece.
ORIGINAL PRICE: $750.00
CURRENT VALUE: $1900.00

Scruffy
24in (61cm) fully-jointed bear in mohair. Blue and white striped bow.
ORIGINAL PRICE: $500.00
CURRENT VALUE: $1275.00

Goldie
16in (41cm) fully-jointed bear in mohair.
INTRODUCED: 1988
PRODUCTION: 5
ORIGINAL PRICE: $130.00
CURRENT VALUE: $275.00

Ted
20in (51cm) fully-jointed teddy produced in domestic plush. Wears vest and hat.
INTRODUCED: 1987
PRODUCTION: One-of-a-kind
ORIGINAL PRICE: $56.00
CURRENT VALUE: $125.00

Monell
14in (36cm) bear in gold wavy mohair. Fully jointed.
INTRODUCED: 1988
PRODUCTION: 4
ORIGINAL PRICE: $125.00
CURRENT VALUE: $275.00

SEIPLE, EDDA

R.D. 2, Box 32
Wrightsville, Pennsylvania 17368
TRADE NAME: River Hills Bears
Edda produced cloth dolls for many years before turning her talents to teddy bears. As a collector for years it was a challenge to design and make a teddy but one she accepted with the birth of her granddaughter. It was years later before she was able to produce a bear that met her expectations.
Photographs by Edda Seiple.

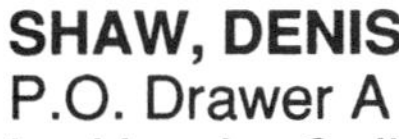

Yoto
Bear on all fours 11in (28cm) long, 7½in (19cm) tall. Produced in mohair. Upholstery fabric for paw pads and inner ears. Safety eyes. Also produced in German synthetic fabric.
INTRODUCED: 1988
PRODUCTION: Limited Edition 300
ORIGINAL PRICE: $70.00
CURRENT VALUE: $150.00

SHAW, DENIS
P.O. Drawer A
La Honda, California 94020
TRADE NAME: Denis's Den
Denis studied art at the San Francisco Art Institute, and in the museums of Europe with subjects including print making, illustration, photography and crafts. Drawing on his training and experience, Denis has discovered the wonderful world of animals, and in particular bears. He learned to make a teddy bear from a friend, and his first animals became gifts and raffle items for local causes. He is continually studying animals in national parks, at the zoo or in the woods, and his enjoyment comes from designing a new pattern. *Photograph by Denis Shaw.*

SHUM, LINDA SUZANNE
226 Willowbrook Ave.
Stamford, Connecticut 06902
TRADE NAME: Ted E. Tail Originals
Linda, who has painted and sewed since elementary school, has always loved the arts. Her career as a teddy bear artist started in 1982 with production help from her husband and mother. Linda's work has appeared on calendars, greeting cards, newspapers, magazines and in books.

Tobias
17in (43cm) fully-jointed bear in acrylic. Cotter pin joints. Musical.
INTRODUCED: 1984
PRODUCTION: 64
ORIGINAL PRICE: $120.00
CURRENT VALUE: $375.00

Jamie
10in (25cm) mohair bear, fully jointed. Wool overalls, cotton t-shirts.
INTRODUCED: 1986
PRODUCTION: 21
ORIGINAL PRICE: $96.00
CURRENT VALUE: $275.00

Just Jesting
12in (31cm) fully-jointed (including tail) in hand dyed mohair.
INTRODUCED: 1986
PRODUCTION: Limited Edition 50
ORIGINAL PRICE: $120.00
CURRENT VALUE: $375.00

Just Friends
12in (31cm) fully-jointed (including tail). Head and paws in llama, body in mohair, hand dyed.
INTRODUCED: 1987
PRODUCTION: Limited Edition 50
ORIGINAL PRICE: $160.00
CURRENT VALUE: $450.00

SOURS, MONTY AND JOE

Rt. 1, Box 40
Golden City, Missouri 64748
TRADE NAME: The Bear Lady

Monty and Joe began making collector teddy bears in 1981. Before the first bear was produced, over a year was spent studying existing designs, both antique and modern. The Sours have incorporated some features of real bears in their designs, while capturing the warm cuddliness of the teddy bear. Monty and Joe attend shows throughout the country, and their bears are also sold in fine stores in this country and in Europe.

Acrylic Plush Bear
17in (43cm) fully-jointed bear in acrylic plush.
INTRODUCED: 1982
PRODUCTION: 800
ORIGINAL PRICE: $35.00
CURRENT VALUE: $150.00

Mohair Bear
10in (25cm) fully jointed bear produced in mohair.
INTRODUCED: 1986
PRODUCTION: 300
ORIGINAL PRICE: $75.00
CURRENT VALUE: $225.00

Mohair Bear
Fully-jointed 9½in (24cm) teddy in mohair.
INTRODUCED: 1988
PRODUCTION: 200
ORIGINAL PRICE: $80.00
CURRENT VALUE: $200.00

Sargeant T. Bear
22in (56cm) fully-jointed bear produced in mohair and wool.
PRODUCTION: Limited Edition 50
ORIGINAL PRICE: $185.00
CURRENT VALUE: $500.00

Anna
5in (13cm) fully-jointed teddy in nylon velvet upholstery fabric, wearing a bear coat and muff, leather boots, scarf and ear muffs. Golden Teddy award winner.
INTRODUCED: 1986
PRODUCTION: Open Edition
ORIGINAL PRICE: $150.00
CURRENT VALUE: $450.00

STEWART, CAROL

903 N.W. Spruce Ridge Dr.
Stuart, Florida 34994

TRADE NAME: Custom Teddy Bears

Carol has worked in a number of different mediums - building her first doll house in 1982 and making miniature toys, although her specialization was in wood carved puppets and stuffed teddy bears. In 1990 Carol was admitted as a Fellow in the International Guild of Miniature Artisans. She is a member of several other related organizations, and has received numerous awards, including a Golden Teddy award as well as being nominated for two TOBY® awards. *Photographs by Carol Stewart.*

The Professor
2⅞in (5cm) tall fully-jointed bear. A miniature copy of the Michauds' ***Professor bear*** in their museum collection. Produced in nylon upholstery velvet. Black knit sweater with red check bow. Painted metal eyes.
INTRODUCED: 1988
PRODUCTION: Open Edition
ORIGINAL PRICE: $100.00
CURRENT VALUE: $250.00

DIANE
2¼in (6cm) string-jointed bear in upholstery velvet.
INTRODUCED: 1988
PRODUCTION: Limited Edition 200
ORIGINAL PRICE: $130.00
CURRENT VALUE: $325.00

Kim
3¼in (8cm) fully-jointed Panda with open mouth. Produced in nylon velvet upholstery fabric.
INTRODUCED: 1986
PRODUCTION: Limited Edition 50
ORIGINAL PRICE: $100.00
CURRENT VALUE: $325.00

BETTY SUAREZ

4030 W. Edison
Tulsa, Oklahoma 74127

TRADE NAME: Bears, Bears and Bears

Betty is an Oklahoma Cherokee, currently living part time in Houston, Texas. She has been designing and making bears since the late 1970s known for her miniature teddies, although in recent years her larger bears have begun to find homes with collectors. Betty prefers the traditional teddy look and makes very few dressed bears. The face is the feature she most loves, whether on her designs or on bears she collects. Betty attends about three conventions a year, enabling her to exchange ideas with artists, add to her collection, meet old friends and make new ones.

Bee Bee
13in (33cm) fully-jointed teddy in golden honey distressed mohair.
INTRODUCED: 1987
PRODUCTION: 20
ORIGINAL PRICE: $85.00
CURRENT VALUE: $225.00

Muffins
15in (38cm) fully-jointed teddy in sheared beaver. Ultra suede nose.
INTRODUCED: 1987
PRODUCTION: 2
ORIGINAL PRICE: $200.00
CURRENT VALUE: $525.00

SWANSON, JUDITH

P.O. Box 6092
Rockford, Illinois 61125-1092
TRADE NAME: Fur Real Bears

Thirty years of experience in design and constructing clothing has been most beneficial to Judy in creating teddy bears, but she discovered that making bears is much more fun. She has a strong appreciation for real furs, which prompted the creation of a teddy bear utilizing real fur. Friends admired her first bear and asked for one of their own, so her business was assured. Each bear produced by Judy is unique in that the variations in color textures and length of hair can never be exactly duplicated. *Photographs by Judith Swanson.*

Bandit
18in (46cm) fully-jointed bear in raccoon fur.
INTRODUCED: 1988
PRODUCTION: Limited Edition 10
ORIGINAL PRICE: $275.00
CURRENT VALUE: $675.00

Loren B. Bear
12in (31cm) fully-jointed teddy. Early models made in acrylic, later in mohair. Handknit vest with penny in pocket.
INTRODUCED: 1981
PRODUCTION: Open Edition
ORIGINAL PRICE: $90.00 (mohair)
CURRENT VALUE: $300.00 (mohair)

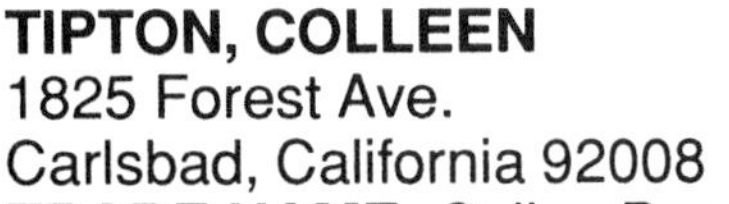

TIPTON, COLLEEN

1825 Forest Ave.
Carlsbad, California 92008
TRADE NAME: Collee Bears

Colleen came by her love of teddy bears from her parents, Wally and Linda Mullins, show promoters and authors. They started Colleen collecting bears around 1976, and in 1980 she attempted her first handcrafted teddy. Colleen has preferred to keep her business on a small scale, so she can work at home and be with her family. *Photographs by Linda Mullins.*

Baby Collee
10in (25cm) fully-jointed bear. Early models in acrylic, later in mohair.
INTRODUCED: 1982
PRODUCTION: Open Edition
ORIGINAL PRICE: $65.00
CURRENT VALUE: $200.00

TOMLINSON, PATRICIA
P.O. Box 3192
Parramatta 2150 N.S.W.
AUSTRALIA
TRADE NAME: Oz-Born Collectibles
This Australian artist made soft toys while still in college to give her some pocket money. Pat also taught craft and needle work for many years and was often called to design various animals and theatre props. Making bears in particular started in 1985. Her bears range in size from 1in (3cm) to five foot high.

Coffee Cream
10in (25cm) fully-jointed bear produced in wool/mohair vintage fabric.
INTRODUCED: 1988
PRODUCTION: Limited Edition 10
ORIGINAL PRICE: $65.00
CURRENT VALUE: $150.00

Miniature Bears
3in (8cm) fully-jointed bear.
INTRODUCED: 1988
ORIGINAL PRICE: $30.00
CURRENT VALUE: $60.00

TROXEL, BARBARA A.
Rt. 1, Box 48
Muscoda, Wisconsin 53573
TRADE NAME: Bear Den Hollow
A former hairdresser and crafter, Barbara learned to sew from her Grandmother Ruby nearly 30 years ago, but has only been making teddy bears since 1984. Working in a modern log home that she and her husband built over a decade ago, Barbara enjoys a flexible schedule that allows her to "fit in" time for her busy teenagers' music and sports events. Barbara enjoys getting away to do antiquing and to attend teddy bear shows.

Treetop Angel Bear
A treetop bear 10in (25cm) high. Head and arms are mohair; body, wings and dress of ecru muslin and eyelet with three laces. Light blue glass ornament tied to wrist with ribbon. Blue satin rosebud in ear.
INTRODUCED: 1987
PRODUCTION: Limited Edition 100
ORIGINAL PRICE: $39.95
CURRENT VALUE: $100.00

Bear Heart
16in (41cm) fully-jointed teddy dressed in romper. Produced in mohair.
INTRODUCED: 1987
PRODUCTION: Open Edition
ORIGINAL PRICE: $75.00
CURRENT VALUE: $175.00

Tattered Teddy
16in (41cm) fully-jointed bear, excelsior stuffing. Produced in mohair. Antique quilt top bib trimmed with vintage lace.
INTRODUCED: 1988
PRODUCTION: Open Edition
ORIGINAL PRICE: $75.00
CURRENT VALUE: $150.00

TURNER, LAURA
1940 Old Taneytown Rd.
Westminster, Maryland 21158
TRADE NAME: Windsor Cottage Crafts
Laura's first attempt at bear making was a small corduroy teddy. Today she works in mohair and old fabrics and bear making has become a full-time vocation. Laura's designs are influenced by her love of antique dolls and toys, with the bears expressing a warm, nostalgic appearance. Her designs also include rabbits and hand painted cloth dolls. *Photographs by Laura Turner.*

Cumberland Bear
17in (43cm) fully-jointed traditional bear, produced in a variety of colors in mohair. Signed, dated and numbered.
INTRODUCED: 1986
PRODUCTION: Limited Edition 100
ORIGINAL PRICE: $90.00
CURRENT VALUE: $250.00

VEINS, MARGARET

14 Ridge Rd.
Waterville, Maine 04901
TRADE NAME: Rak-A-Ree-Bos

Since Margaret made her first bear as a Christmas gift for her twin sister in 1983, she has personally designed and created over 3000 bears for collectors everywhere. Her bears range in size from 5in (13cm) to 36in (91cm). In the fall of 1991 Margaret semi-retired from actively producing bears and is now making less than 100 bears per year. Her trade name "Rak-A-Ree-Bos" is an old Maine Yankee expression her grandfather had for "little animals in the woods you might hear but do not see." *Photographs by Margaret Veins.*

Christmas Edition Bears
13in (33cm) fully-jointed bears in golden tan mohair. Santa has pot belly under his white beard. Red velvet pants held up by suspenders. Glasses. Mrs. Claws wears lace trimmed white pantaloons under a Christmas print dress topped by an eyelet apron and cap. She is working on a quilt.
INTRODUCED: 1988
PRODUCTION: Limited Edition 12 sets
ORIGINAL PRICE: $125.00 each
CURRENT VALUE: $300.00 each

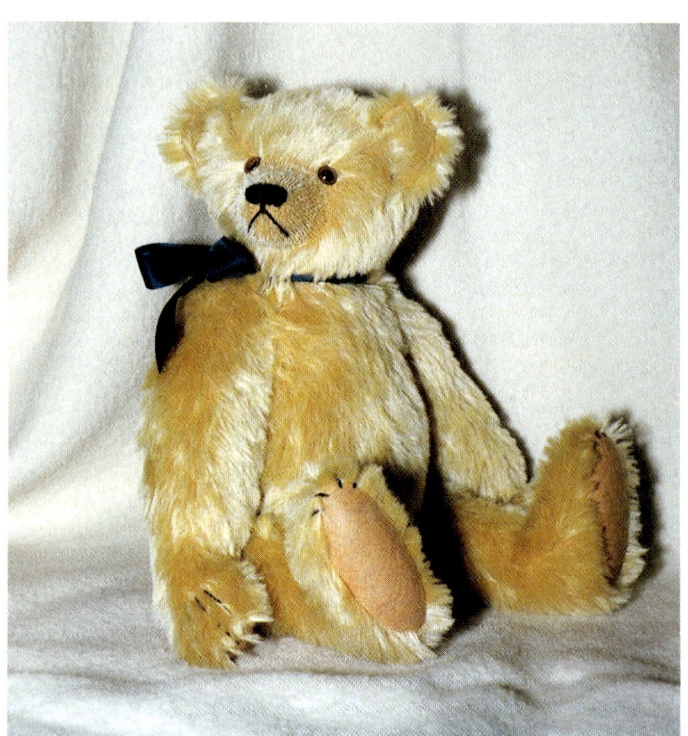

Rufus
15in (38cm) fully-jointed bear in mohair. Growler.
INTRODUCED: 1987
ORIGINAL PRICE: $95.00
CURRENT VALUE: $250.00

WALLACE, KATHLEEN

2121 Main St.
Narvon, Pennsylvania 17555
TRADE NAME: Stier Bears

Kathy has been sewing since she was a young girl and making teddy bears since 1982. She wanted to design and produce a bear for people who could not afford the high prices of antique teddies. In the beginning Kathy used old fabrics, including old coats, antique ticking and upholstery. She sold at craft shows until 1987 when she did her first teddy bear show. It was shortly after that first show that bear making became a full-time business for Kathy, her husband and children, and several friends. *Photographs by Andy Phillips.*

Bethany
Fully-jointed 30in (76cm) bear in mohair. Growler.
INTRODUCED: 1987
PRODUCTION: One-of-a-kind
ORIGINAL PRICE: $225.00
CURRENT VALUE: $600.00

Marcus
24in (61cm) fully-jointed bear. Produced in distressed mohair. Growler.
INTRODUCED: 1987
ORIGINAL PRICE: $150.00
CURRENT VALUE: $400.00

Ryan
17in (43cm) fully-jointed bear with growler. Produced in mohair.
INTRODUCED: 1987
ORIGINAL PRICE: $120.00
CURRENT VALUE: $325.00

Wally
22in (56cm) bear in distressed mohair. Fully jointed. Growler.
INTRODUCED: 1987
PRODUCTION: Limited Edition 150
ORIGINAL PRICE: $175.00
CURRENT VALUE: $475.00

Clarissa
27in (69cm) fully-jointed teddy in mohair. Growler. Antique outfit.
INTRODUCED: 1988
PRODUCTION: One-of-a-kind
ORIGINAL PRICE: $295.00
CURRENT VALUE: $750.00

WARLOW, GERRY
30 John St.
Rosewood 4340 Queensland
Australia
TRADE NAME: Gerry's Teddy and Craft Designs
Gerry lives with her husband and two teenage children in the small country town of Rosewood in Queensland, Australia. She started her bear making in 1983 and after some initial fears of putting joints in bears, Gerry has since created many new and original designs. Gerry finds it extremely rewarding to see one of her new designs come to life.

Paper Boy Bear
3in (8cm) fully-jointed bear in velour. Hand sewn. Bead eyes. Navy velour pants, red velour cap. Calico bag containing papers and sling shot.
PRODUCTION: 25
ORIGINAL PRICE: $30.00
CURRENT VALUE: $75.00

School Boy Bear
3in (8cm) fully-jointed bear in velour. Hand sewn. Bead eyes. Tartan pants. Red felt cap. White collar. Carries fimo apple and bottle containing his insect collection.
PRODUCTION: 7
ORIGINAL PRICE: $30.00
CURRENT VALUE: $75.00

Fyodor
("Theodore" in Russian) 18in (46cm) fully-jointed teddy in mohair. Velveteen paws.
INTRODUCED: 1987
PRODUCTION: Open Edition
ORIGINAL PRICE: $425.00
CURRENT VALUE: $1225.00

WAUGH, CAROL-LYNN RÖSSELL
c/o Morrill St.
Winthrop, Maine 04364
Carol-Lynn wears many hats in the teddy bear world, including designer and teddy bear artist, author of 21 books and hundreds of articles, photographer, designer of collector bears for several manufacturers, pattern designer for Simplicity Pattern Company - to name just a few of her many talents. She also produces a limited number of teddies to sell to collectors herself, all originals made by her. Every Waugh bear wears a heart pendant, including her first mohair bear named "Yetta" designed in 1975. *Photograph by Carol-Lynn Rossell Waugh.*

Prudence
12in (31cm) fully-jointed bear produced in mohair.
PRODUCTION: 10
ORIGINAL PRICE: $95.00
CURRENT VALUE: $250.00

WHISNANT, BARBARA

11160 S.W. Waverly Pl.
Portland, Oregon 97225
TRADE NAME: Barbear and Friends Ltd.
Barbara began making bears to sell in 1984, and her work is sold in a number of shops around the country. Her bears range in size from 6in (15cm) to 30in (76cm). Barbara has two grown children, and she lives in Portland with her husband. Barbara says her husband is her advisor, number one supporter, and a great help in the kitchen after dinner, which allows her to work a few more hours. Barbara also enjoys yard work, giving bear talks, church work, power walking and playing tennis. *Photographs by Barbara Whisnant.*

Jesterbear
16in (41cm) fully-jointed mohair bear. Music Box.
PRODUCTION: 197
ORIGINAL PRICE: $90.00
CURRENT VALUE: $225.00

WHITE, BEV

399 Echo Dell Rd.
Downingtown, Pennsylvania 19335
TRADE NAME: Happy Tymes Collectables
Like many teddy bear artists, Bev began as a doll maker. She needed three bears to go with Goldilocks, and from that point on it was a love affair with the teddy bear. Her first bears in 1986 were constructed from wool fabrics, utilizing a pattern in a magazine. After making a few plush bears, Bev quickly discovered the beauty of mohair, and now she works in that fabric almost exclusively.

Lady Libearty
18in (46cm) fully-jointed bear in wool fabric.
INTRODUCED: 1986
PRODUCTION: 3
ORIGINAL PRICE: $75.00
CURRENT VALUE: $200.00

Beary Shy Bear
12in (31cm) fully-jointed bear in pink mohair. Lace collar. Accompanied by a cotton comforter.
INTRODUCED: 1988
PRODUCTION: Open Edition
ORIGINAL PRICE: $75.00
CURRENT VALUE: $150.00

Say Your Prayers
6in (15cm) fully-jointed teddy in gold mohair. Leather foot pads.
INTRODUCED: 1988
PRODUCTION: Open Edition
ORIGINAL PRICE: $50.00
CURRENT VALUE: $100.00

WOESSNER, JOAN
P.O. Box 27920
Escondido, California 92027
TRADE NAME: Bear Elegance
Joan and her husband, Mike, operate their business from their studio in California, where their family and friends assist them. They began in 1986, and today are shipping bears throughout the United States and Europe. Joan's designs are instantly recognizable by their touch of mink for eyelashes, giving them a very distinct appearance. Joan and Mike find making bears very rewarding, and they are very pleased with the many friends they have made, in both collector circles and teddy bear stores. *Photographs by Larry McDaniel.*

Peaches
12in (31cm) fully-jointed teddy in synthetic plush fabric. Pellet stuffed.
PRODUCTION: 53
ORIGINAL PRICE: $64.00
CURRENT VALUE: $150.00

Rosie
7in (18cm) fully-jointed bag lady bear. Alpaca fabric. Vintage camel coat.
PRODUCTION: 35
ORIGINAL PRICE: $100.00
CURRENT VALUE: $275.00

Teddy Goodbar
18in (46cm) fully-jointed teddy in German synthetic fabric. Fimo claws.
PRODUCTION: 60
ORIGINAL PRICE: $175.00
CURRENT VALUE: $425.00

OPPOSITE PAGE:
TOP:
Cinnamon
11½in (29cm) fully-jointed bear in mohair fabric. Pellet stuffed.
PRODUCTION: Open Edition
ORIGINAL PRICE: $84.00
CURRENT VALUE: $200.00

BOTTOM LEFT:
Jeffrey
13½in (34cm) fully-jointed bear in merino wool. Pellet stuffed.
PRODUCTION: 35
ORIGINAL PRICE: $130.00
CURRENT VALUE: $325.00

BOTTOM RIGHT:
Carmel
12in (31cm) mohair bear, pellet stuffed. Fully jointed.
PRODUCTION: Open Edition
ORIGINAL PRICE: $88.00
CURRENT VALUE: $200.00

WOOLEY, PAMELA
5021 Stringtown Rd.
Evansville, Indiana 47711
TRADE NAME: Wooley Bear Cottage
Pamela has been designing and creating teddies since 1984. She started collecting manufactured bears, but she was displeased with the workmanship, and it led her to design and produce her own. Pamela does all of the work in bringing her teddies to life, an important fact to her, as she considers collector bears to be works of art which deserve personal attention. It gives her great satisfaction to know that her teddies have gone to live with arctophiles all over the world, and that their soulful expressions have touched so many hearts. What could be more enjoyable than having a profession in which you are able to create gentle, loving teddies that make people smile. *Photographs by Richard Wooley.*

Baxter
17in (43cm) fully-jointed bear in wavy mohair. Constructed with arms behind back.
PRODUCTION: Limited Edition 25
ORIGINAL PRICE: $265.00
CURRENT VALUE: $650.00

Roosevelt
18in (46cm) and 22in (56cm) bears in distressed mohair. Fully jointed. Antique shoe button eyes.
PRODUCTION: Limited Edition 10 (18in); Open Edition (22in)
ORIGINAL PRICE: $250.00 (18in); $275.00 (22in)
CURRENT VALUE: $600.00 (18in); $675.00 (22in)

Chelsea
13in (33cm) fully-jointed bear in 1in (3cm) mohair. Country calico dress. Basket of hand dyed flowers.
PRODUCTION: Limited Edition 20
ORIGINAL PRICE: $250.00
CURRENT VALUE: $625.00

Limited Edition Mohair Bear
15in (38cm) fully-jointed bear produced in three colors of mohair. Safety locked plexiglass eyes.
INTRODUCED: 1984
PRODUCTION: Limited Edition 300
ORIGINAL PRICE: $150.00
CURRENT VALUE: $525.00

WRIGHT, BEVERLY MARTIN

890 Patrol Rd.
Woodside, California 94062
TRADE NAME: The Wright Bear
As a child, Bev loved sewing and drawing and even majored in art at college. In 1980, with her children grown, she began to look for more creative work than her legal transcription business. Since her hobby-made jointed bears had sold at Christmas fairs, attending other craft shows and finally bear shows in 1984 was a logical choice. As of 1986 Bev had dedicated more time to making bears to be sold through stores rather than at shows.

WRIGHT, NAN

509 Olinda Ave.
Des Moines, Iowa 50315
TRADE NAME: Olde Tyme Toys and Treasures
Nan Wright turned her bear making hobby into a full-time business over a decade ago. With a love of the outdoors, it is no wonder that Nan's bears appear more like real bears with their open mouths and leather claws. Her background as a portrait artist is also reflected in her work. Many of Nan's bears have won first place honors including Golden Teddy awards in 1987 and 1988. *Photographs by Nan Wright.*

Kris
15in (38cm) fully-jointed teddy in mohair. Leather nose and paws. Removable wool beard and eyebrows. Wears fur trimmed red wool hooded cloak. Bendable arms.
INTRODUCED: 1986
PRODUCTION: Limited Edition 12
ORIGINAL PRICE: $300.00
CURRENT VALUE: $900.00

Stoney a.k.a. Ace
26in (66cm) fully-jointed bear in imported fur. Wears leather flight jacket with sheepskin collar, white scarf and aviator wings.
INTRODUCED: 1987
PRODUCTION: Limited Edition 20
ORIGINAL PRICE: $300.00
CURRENT VALUE: $750.00

Applejack
26in (66cm) fully-jointed bear in brown frosted fur. Open red leather mouth and tongue. Brown leather nose and paws.
INTRODUCED: 1984
PRODUCTION: Open Edition
ORIGINAL PRICE: $150.00
CURRENT VALUE: $500.00

Christopher
16in (41cm) fully-jointed bear produced in off-white alpaca. Pellet stuffed. Choir-boy collar in black velvet with wide satin bow and trimmed in hand-tatted lace.
INTRODUCED: 1988
PRODUCTION: Open Edition
ORIGINAL PRICE: $145.00
CURRENT VALUE: $350.00

ZIMMERMAN, MARIE

W. 8676 Stevenson Dr.
Poynette, Wisconsin 53955

TRADE NAME: Paw Quette

Marie has a degree in Veterinary Technology and has worked in the veterinary field since 1979, although sewing and costume design are her first loves. She maintains that all of her course work in anatomy and physiology has greatly helped her in pattern design. She even closes her bears using surgical closure "sutures." She often gets comments from customers about the similarity between the faces of her bears and the faces of "lost puppies." Bear making took over her professional life, and Marie left the veterinary field to devote her time to bear design and making.

SECTION TWO

MANUFACTURED COLLECTOR TEDDY BEARS

This section contains a listing of teddy bears which may have been designed by an artist, but have been produced by someone other than the artist.

Please note that in the case of open edition bears, or bears still available, the current value listed applies only to the bears produced during the year of introduction, and only to those in mint condition with all original boxes, certificates and tags. Teddy bears of the same issue produced in subsequent years, or in condition less than original, would reflect a current value of a lower amount.

BEARLY THERE, INC.

14782 Moran St.
Westminster, California 92683-5553

Bearly There, Inc. had its beginnings in 1976 when founder/designer Linda Spiegel Lohre began making teddy bears with two friends. Jane Martell and Betty Grime each contributed greatly to Linda's learning process and bear making became a total enjoyment for Linda. When Linda's granddaughter came to live with her, the garage was converted into a mini bear factory so that more time could be spent at home.

Linda started with a commercial sewing machine, 55 yards of brown acrylic plush fabric, and one part-time employee. After a year of operating in her garage, Linda moved her operation into a little corner in the back of a friend's warehouse. Two more employees were hired, and a sales representative started to offer her bears to wholesale accounts.

In 1983 Linda's former husband wanted to buy her out, but Linda's father Leslie D. Truman formed a partnership with her, and they set out to build a bigger bear company. After moving into larger quarters and hiring more employees, business went down instead of up. More sales representatives were hired, and the unique designs of Bearly There were soon being shown in most of the major trade shows. Another factor in turning the business

1979 School Bear
14in (36cm) fully-jointed bear, first original bear designed by Linda Spiegel. Acrylic plush. Dressed in bright shirt, suspenders, blue or brown trousers. Early models had plastic noses, later changed to embroidered noses.
ORIGINAL PRICE: $50.50
CURRENT VALUE: $450.00

1981 Summer
14in (36cm) fully-jointed bear in camel color acrylic plush. Bear was made in honor of Linda's granddaughter and is one of a very few Bearly There models with a smile. Wears pink sunsuit with pink bow in each ear.
ORIGINAL PRICE: $50.00
CURRENT VALUE: $325.00

around was a brand new design by Linda that took the bear world by storm. It was their new ***Gus*** line. ***Gus*** was a totally new departure from the traditional teddy bear. He had big humped shoulders, a very large tummy, uniquely bent arms, and short legs. When ***Gus*** was introduced, orders started to flow in.

Tragedy struck the firm with the passing of Linda's father Leslie. He was so loved by all the bear makers that it was difficult for them to function without his guidance. It was his wish that Linda's sister Marie McMurran become part of the company. Marie joined the firm and contributed greatly in much the same way their father had. Linda says that Marie has her father's wisdom, good sense and his mildness. Marie is the steady influence when all seems to be going wrong.

Bearly There, Inc. has continued to grow, and Linda is convinced that Leslie's influence is still being felt. Orders are being shipped throughout the United States and to Japan and Europe. Linda feels fulfilled in her design and bear making business. She still manages to do much of the finish work on the bears in spite of a hectic schedule of personal appearances throughout the country. She also cherishes her time with her husband Jeffery Lohre, her three grown children and three wonderful grandchildren.

Basil
15in (38cm) fully-jointed bear in acrylic plush. Assorted colors.
ORIGINAL PRICE: $51.50
CURRENT VALUE: $325.00

1982 Bradie
26in (66cm) fully-jointed bear in acrylic.
ORIGINAL PRICE: $90.00
CURRENT VALUE: $500.00

1984 Buttercup
15in (38cm) fully-jointed bear produced in sheep wool acrylic. Shoe button eyes. Horizontal stitched nose.
ORIGINAL PRICE: $70.00
CURRENT VALUE:
$275.00

Silly Old Bear
8½in (22cm) fully-jointed bear in gold color upholstery fabric. Embroidered nose, mouth, and eyebrows. Wooden eyes.
ORIGINAL PRICE: $51.50
CURRENT VALUE:
$200.00

Norbert No No
11in (28cm) bear in camel color acrylic plush. Arms and legs jointed. Head moves "No No" by turning tail. Taffeta clown hat and ruff around neck. Two color clown suit in assorted colors.
ORIGINAL PRICE: $50.00
CURRENT VALUE:
$200.00

1985 Holy Jim
11in (28cm) bear jointed at arms and legs. Produced in various color acrylic plush. Patches on body. Artist signed and dated.
ORIGINAL PRICE: $52.50
CURRENT VALUE: $200.00

Pom Pom
13in (33cm) fully-jointed bear in heather green and white clown suit. Pattern actually consisted of 29 pieces. Gold acrylic head. Cotton white pom pom on head. Hand pinked white felt ruffle around neck and leg cuffs.
ORIGINAL PRICE: $150.00
CURRENT VALUE: $600.00

Understanding Emery
25in (64cm) fully-jointed bear in long cream color acrylic plush. Shaved snout. Red bow on neck.
ORIGINAL PRICE: $150.00
CURRENT VALUE: $550.00

1986 Mr. Honeywell and His Golli
15in (38cm) bear in camel acrylic, jointed arms and legs. 1930s style yellow and brown striped jacket. ***Golli*** is a 10in (25cm) rag doll with embroidered face.
PRODUCTION: Limited Edition 30
ORIGINAL PRICE: $160.00 set
CURRENT VALUE: $550.00 set

1987 Tex and His Bare Behind
13in (33cm) bear jointed arms and legs. Produced in company's popular ***Gus*** pattern. Mocha acrylic. Wears red union suit with back flap open on one side. Rumpled tea-dyed straw hat, handkerchief around neck. Holds Lone Star tobacco pouch hand drawn by Linda Spiegel Lohre.
ORIGINAL PRICE: $73.00
CURRENT VALUE: $200.00

Eureka
15in (38cm) fully-jointed bear produced in various color acrylic plush. Shaved snout.
ORIGINAL PRICE: $71.00
CURRENT VALUE: $200.00

ALGERNON
14in (36cm) fully-jointed bear in off-white upholstery fabric. Dressed in black English walking suit and cap. Wears monocle and carries walking stick. Part of a set (See ***Penelope***).
ORIGINAL PRICE: $100.00
CURRENT VALUE: $275.00

Penelope
14in (36cm) fully-jointed bear in upholstery fabric, dressed in fur-trimmed matching walking suit. Wears rimless glasses and hat. Part of a set (see ***Algernon***).
ORIGINAL PRICE: $100.00
CURRENT VALUE: $275.00

1988 Treasure Ted
15in (38cm) fully-jointed bear in distressed tan mohair. Fabric distressed by artist.
PRODUCTION: Limited Edition 200
ORIGINAL PRICE: $250.00
CURRENT VALUE: $650.00

Remembering Truman
13in (33cm) bear with jointed arms and legs. Produced in extra long gray brown acrylic plush. This bear was designed and produced in memory of Linda's father Leslie D. Truman and is dressed in a costume their father wore to a Halloween party. Wears glasses and a red and white dotted tie. Grocery list and reminder to "call mom" attached to tie with clothespin. String tied around finger as a reminder to always remember Truman.
PRODUCTION: Limited Edition 75
ORIGINAL PRICE: $58.00
CURRENT VALUE: $175.00

Homer
13in (33cm) fully-jointed bear in camel color acrylic. Wears "Babe Ruth" type baseball uniform with team name "Bears". Carries hand made baseball glove.
ORIGINAL PRICE: $150.00
CURRENT VALUE: $350.00

Spanky
15in (38cm) fully-jointed bear in camel acrylic. Pellet stuffed. Wears red or blue t-shirt, twisted suspenders, brown knickers. Holds sling shot. Earliest ***Spankys*** had antique buttons on felt beanie, later replaced with new buttons. A few special orders were polyfil stuffed.
ORIGINAL PRICE: $79.00
CURRENT VALUE: $150.00

1989 Geraldine
9in (23cm) fully-jointed bear in gold acrylic plush. Wooden bead eyes. Wears shiny gold cone cap with pom poms on it. Ruff on neck.
PRODUCTION: Limited Edition 25
ORIGINAL PRICE: $64.00
CURRENT VALUE: $150.00

BLESSED COMPANION BEAR COMPANY

7160 S.W. Fir Loop #100
Tigard, Oregon 97223-8722

The **Blessed Companion Bear Company** is a worldwide guild of artisans founded in 1986, inspired by the humor and wisdom of Sri Da Avabhasa. The unique creations of these artisans are recognized by their unusual molded wax or resin faces, some of the very few molded face teddy bears being produced today. The artisans are guided by sculptural skills of the founder of the company, Nanci Seely/Van Roozendall.

The English tradition of wax doll making provided the basis for these bears to make their debut in 1988. The introduction of the line was preceded by several years of research and experimentation. The wax has a warm translucent quality that can be dyed and painted, adding depth to each individual character. Although wax has some limitations (vulnerability to scratches and bruises), Nanci and her group feel that its uniqueness will be appreciated by collectors who look for features not yet found in other bears.

In 1990, as their never ending search for new materials continued, they added resin molded faces. It has the warm appearance of wax, but is much more durable for the collector who wants more hands-on participation with their bear.

The response to the Blessed Companion Bear Company's line has been extremely gratifying to Nanci and her staff. In their short history, they have already been nominated twice for a TOBY® award. They also have received praise for their construction, design excellence and creativity from collectors and artists alike. As for the future, this group of talented artists will continue their search for new techniques to enhance the marvelous qualities of the teddy.

Bodhi, Kukui and Harp
A trio of bears that began the molded face process for the Blessed Companion Bear Company. Designed by Nanci Seely/Van Roozendaal. ***Bodhi*** and ***Harp*** are 9in (23cm), ***Kukui*** is 8in (23cm) tall. All produced in mohair fabric. Also produced in resin face.
INTRODUCED: 1988
PRODUCTION: Limited Edition 500 each design
ORIGINAL PRICE: $285.00 each (***Bodhi*** and ***Harp*** — wax face); $210.00 each (***Bodhi*** and ***Harp*** — resin face); $260 (***Kukui*** — wax face); $185 (***Kukui*** — resin face)
CURRENT VALUE: $825.00 (***Bodhi*** and ***Harp*** — wax face); $600.00 (***Bodhi*** and ***Harp*** — resin face); $750.00 (***Kukui*** — wax face); $525.00 (***Kukui*** — resin face)

Papa, Mama and Little Booja
Mama and Papa 11in (28cm) tall, ***Little Booja*** 7in (18cm) tall. Produced in German acrylic plush. Available in wax or resin face. Designed by Nanci Seely/Van Roozendaal.
INTRODUCED: 1989
PRODUCTION: Limited Edition 500 each design

ORIGINAL PRICE:: $300.00 each (***Papa*** and ***Mama*** — wax face); $225.00 each (***Papa*** and ***Mama*** — resin face); $270.00 (***Little Booja*** — wax face); $195.00 (***Little Booja*** — resin face)
CURRENT VALUE: $725.00 each (***Papa*** and ***Mama*** — wax face); $525.00 each (***Papa*** and ***Mama*** — resin face); $650.00 (***Little Booja*** — wax face); $475.00 (***Little Booja*** — resin face)

Wagner The Nerd
11in (28cm) tall in German acrylic plush. Designed by Lydia DePole.
INTRODUCED: 1989
PRODUCTION: Limited Edition 100
ORIGINAL PRICE: $375.00 (wax face); $300.00 (resin face)
CURRENT VALUE: $925.00 (wax face); $725.00 (resin face)

Zeno The Philosopher
9in (23cm) bear in alpaca fabric. Designed by Nanci Seely/Van Roozendaal. Carries handwoven Guatemalan lean-to.
INTRODUCED: 1989
PRODUCTION: Limited Edition 500
ORIGINAL PRICE: $300.00 (wax face); $225.00 (resin face)
CURRENT VALUE: $725.00 (wax face); $525.00 (resin face)

Sushi The Sumo
9in (23cm) bear produced in leather. Wears Japanese kimono and hand woven loin cloth. Designed by Nanci Seely/Van Roozendaal.
INTRODUCED: 1989
PRODUCTION: Limited Edition 100
ORIGINAL PRICE: $450.00 (wax face); $375.00 (resin face)
CURRENT VALUE: $1100.00 (wax face); $925.00 (resin face)

CANTERBURY BEARS, LTD.
Littlebourne, Canterbury
England

Although a comparatively new producer of teddy bears, this British company has had a rapid growth and wide acceptance throughout the world. The company actually started in the family home at Westbere in 1980. Founders are Maude and John Blackburn, and it was John who had been commissioned to design a fully-jointed traditional teddy bear in the latter part of 1979. In January 1981 their initial designs were shown for the first time at the Earls Court Toy Fair in London.

In 1984 the company moved to their present studio/workshop in Littlebourne, a small village located just four miles from the beautiful ancient city of Canterbury. The workshops occupy what was once a mushroom farm and are surrounded by large apple and pear orchards. It was our privilege to visit their facilities with Keystone Traders, Ltd. first British Teddy Tour, and we have repeated our visit every year since. Maude, John and their family and employees are always outstanding hosts to our group, and it has become one of the highlights of our annual visit to England.

Canterbury Bears is very much a family business and each member of the family is firmly committed to the pursuit of excellence which is reflected in the reputation that the company has built since its founding. Canterbury Bears was recently selected by the famous Gund Corporation to produce an exclusive line of Canterbury Bears now distributed by Gund, Inc. in the United States. There is also a Canterbury Bear Collectors Society, formed in 1990. (See **Information Please section.**)

Maude and John Blackburn make frequent personal appearances throughout the United States, including the popular **Walt Disney World® Teddy Bear and Doll Convention** held each December in Florida.

1983

Peter (designed by John)
6in (15cm) bears made in assorted colors in mohair, alpaca or wool.
PRODUCTION: Open Edition
ORIGINAL PRICE: $25.00
CURRENT VALUE: $125.00

Edward Nut (designed by John)
14in (36cm) fully-jointed bear produced in mod-acrylic Belgium fibre. Suede paws.
PRODUCTION: Open Edition
ORIGINAL PRICE: $38.00
CURRENT VALUE: $175.00

1984

Mr. and Mrs. Berwick (designed by John)
Mr. Berwick 21in (53cm) and ***Mrs. Berwick*** 18in (46cm) produced in black mod-acrylic Belgium fabric. Contains slight silver fleck.
PRODUCTION: Open Edition
ORIGINAL PRICE: $60.00 (***Mr. Berwick***); $45.00 (***Mrs. Berwick***)
CURRENT VALUE: $225.00 (***Mr. Berwick***); $175.00 (***Mrs. Berwick***)

1985

Dressing Gown Bear (designed by Maude)
Produced in small 12in (31cm) and large 19in (48cm) sizes. Unique design with the bear and the dressing gown made of the same pure wool fabric.
PRODUCTION: Open Edition
ORIGINAL PRICE: $45.00 (12in); $80.00 (19in)
CURRENT VALUE: $150.00 (12in); $275.00 (19in)

1986

Arran Bear (designed by Maude)
15in (38cm) fully-jointed bear in Belgium mod-acrylic fabric. Sweater, trousers, scarf and hat are handknitted Arran by local Kentish women.
PRODUCTION: Open Edition
ORIGINAL PRICE: $60.00
CURRENT VALUE: $175.00

Check Bear (designed by Maude)
16in (41cm) fully-jointed bear produced of hand made Indian cotton patchwork. Individually cut pieces facilitate the matching of the checks.
PRODUCTION: Limited Edition 35
ORIGINAL PRICE: $65.00
CURRENT VALUE: $225.00

Honey Bear (designed by John)
12in (31cm) fully-jointed bear in short German mohair.
PRODUCTION: Open Edition
ORIGINAL PRICE: $85.00
CURRENT VALUE: $275.00

1987

Harrods Bear (designed by John)
This bear was specially designed for an Edwardian Exhibition and produced exclusively for the famous Harrods department store in London. It was made in four sizes; 11in (28cm), 14in (36cm), 21in (53cm) and 26in (66cm) in distressed English mohair with Harrods own ribbon.
PRODUCTION: Open Edition
ORIGINAL PRICE: $28.00 (11in); $40.00 (14in); $70.00 (21in); $125.00 (26in)
CURRENT VALUE: $75.00 (11in); $100.00 (14in); $200.00 (21in); $375.00 (26in)

1988

No Name (designed by Maude)
19in (48cm) fully-jointed bear in pale cream distressed mohair with black Buffalo hide paws, pads and inner ears.
PRODUCTION: Limited Edition 200
ORIGINAL PRICE: $130.00
CURRENT VALUE: $350.00

Tartan Bears
18in (46cm) fully-jointed bear produced in 100% pure wool tartan made in Scotland. Heads made in mohair and alpaca. Made to order in specific tartan.
PRODUCTION: Open Edition
ORIGINAL PRICE: $100.00
CURRENT VALUE: $225.00

1989

Sir Walter (designed by Maude)
12in (31cm) fully-jointed bear produced in pale distressed mohair. Sold only at Epcot Center at Walt Disney World.
PRODUCTION: Limited Edition 50
ORIGINAL PRICE: $100.00
CURRENT VALUE: $225.00

Alexander and Son (designed by John)
Alexander 26in (66cm) and Son 11in (28cm) produced in mohair with cashmere paws and pads with individual padded leather toes.
PRODUCTION: Limited Edition 50
ORIGINAL PRICE: $300.00 set
CURRENT VALUE: $700.00 set

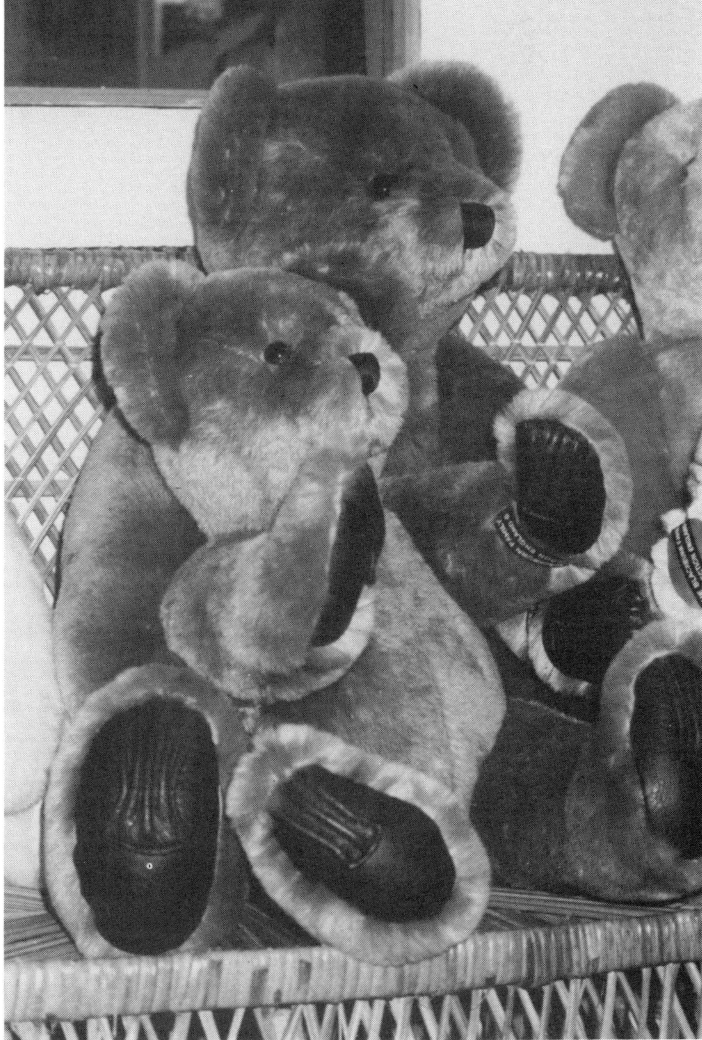

Digby and Son (designed by John)
Digby 34in (86cm) and ***Son*** 28in (71cm) produced in gray long pile mohair with leather paws and pads incorporating handsewn ribbing.
PRODUCTION: Limited Edition: 50
ORIGINAL PRICE: $400.00 set
CURRENT VALUE: $950.00 set

GUND, INC.
P.O. Box H
Edison, New Jersey 08818

Gund, the oldest independent toy company in America, was founded in 1898 in Norwalk, Connecticut by German emigrant Adolph Gund. This historic company has maintained a leadership role in developing innovative and luxurious plush animals for children and adults. In 1925, the **GUND Manufacturing Company** was purchased by Adolph GUND's personal assistant, Jacob Swedlin. It was Swedlin who pioneered industry licensing agreements to produce the first stuffed animal versions of Walt Disney, King Features and Hanna Barbera cartoon characters, including such classics as Mickey Mouse, Pluto, the Pink Panther and Popeye.

In the early 1970s Gund's huggable "Luv-Me-Bear" made toy industry history by introducing the technique of understuffing each animal and using softer materials. Then in the late 1970s Gund's "Collector Classics" became the first line of upscale, uniquely crafted stuffed animals targeting adults and collectors.

A more recent development of interest to collectors is the line of **Canterbury Bears** from Great Britain now imported and distributed in the United States exclusively by Gund. **Canterbury Bears** are fine handcrafted English bears which have a loyal following amongst teddy bear collectors the world over. Special editions created by **Canterbury Bears** for Gund are now enjoying a great acceptance in the United States and Canada.

Another bear that is produced by Gund that has won the hearts of arctophiles everywhere is ***Bialosky Bear***. ***Bialosky*** is not just another bear. He is the proud leader of a whole family of books, stationery and gifts that bring him more devoted friends and admirers every day. It all began in the fall of 1980, with Workman's publication of *The Teddy Bear Catalogue* by Peggy and Alan Bialosky, authoritative teddy bear collectors. Without question, the Bialoskys' work combined with two books by the late Peter Bull, can be credited with sowing the seeds of our present day teddy bear collecting movement. It is true that teddy bears have always been popular with children and adults, but because of the favorable publicity generated by the Bialoskys' book, it became "acceptable" for adults to collect teddy bears. We will always be indebted to these two warm hearted people for sharing the world of the teddy bear with us.

Bialosky Bear is the favored bear in the Bialoskys' extensive collection, and he quickly became the figurehead on a special line of teddy bear items. In 1983 Gund brought their design talents and experience to the introduction of ***Bialosky Bear*** to the collector's world. He has since been presented in various sizes and costumes, and they are eagerly picked up by arctophiles to add to their collections.

Following are the various styles of ***Bialosky Bear*** and their current values, from their introduction in 1983 through the 1990 collection.

1983

The original Bialosky Bear from Peggy and Alan Bialosky's personal collection.

Bialosky Bear #7651 and #7621
Fully-jointed 18in (46cm) and 12in (31cm) bear produced in three outfits; Tuxedo, Golfer, and Sailor.
ORIGINAL PRICE: $48.00 (18in); $25.00 (12in)
CURRENT VALUE: $225.00 (18in); $100.00 (12in)

Bialosky Bear #7600
Three assorted 6½in (17cm) bears, each in their own "Teddy Bear to Go" box. **ORIGINAL PRICE:** $10.00
CURRENT VALUE: $50.00

1984

Gloriosky Bialosky #7670
30in (76cm) limited edition bear wearing red and blue sweater. Each bear is numbered and hand signed by Peggy and Alan Bialosky.
ORIGINAL PRICE: $130.00
CURRENT VALUE: $600.00

12in (31cm) and 18in (46cm) Bialosky Bears in various outfits:
#7624 12in, #7654 18in ***Tuxedo Bialosky*** in white tie and tails
#7622 12in, #7652 18in ***Golfer Bialosky*** in sweater and bow tie
#7623 12in, #7653 18in ***Sailor Bialosky*** in sailor shirt and tie
#7625 12in, #7655 18in ***Santa Bialosky*** in jacket and cap
#7626 12in, #7656 18in ***Skier Bialosky*** in ski sweater
ORIGINAL PRICE: $25.00 (12in); $50.00 (18in)
CURRENT VALUE: $100.00 (12in); $225.00 (18in)

7655 7656

7625 7626

1985

Varsity Bialosky #7615
Softly stuffed (unjointed) 12in (31cm) bear. Handmade sweater with varsity letter. Produced in two colors.
ORIGINAL PRICE: $22.00
CURRENT VALUE: $75.00

Santa Bialosky #7616
Softly stuffed 12in (31cm) bear wearing red cap and sweater.
ORIGINAL PRICE: $22.00
CURRENT VALUE: $75.00

Camper Bialosky #7617
Softly stuffed 12in (31cm) bear. Calendar bear for 1986. Wears camp jacket.
ORIGINAL PRICE: $22.00
CURRENT VALUE: $75.00

Bjorn Bialosky #7632
15½in (39cm) bear softly stuffed, wearing sweater and cap.
ORIGINAL PRICE: $35.00
CURRENT VALUE: $125.00

Camper Bialosky #7634
Same as above in 15½in (39cm) size. Wears jacket and scarf.
ORIGINAL PRICE: $35.00
CURRENT VALUE: $125.00

Country Gentleman Bialosky #7635
15½in (39cm) softly stuffed bear wearing plaid shirt, tie and vest.
ORIGINAL PRICE: $35.00
CURRENT VALUE: $125.00

Bomber Pilot Bialosky #7664
Fully-jointed 18in (46cm) bear in pilot's jacket and scarf.
ORIGINAL PRICE: $53.00
CURRENT VALUE: $200.00

Pierot Bialosky #7657
Fully-jointed 18in (46cm) bear in Pierot costume.
ORIGINAL PRICE: $53.00
CURRENT VALUE: $200.00

Camper Bialosky #7658
Full-jointed 18in (46cm) bear.
ORIGINAL PRICE: $53.00
CURRENT VALUE: $200.00

Gloriosky Bialosky #7686
30in (76cm) limited edition. Calendar bear for 1986. Buckskin paws. Numbered and hand signed by Peggy and Alan Bialosky.
ORIGINAL PRICE: $150.00
CURRENT VALUE: $625.00

Note: In 1985 Gund also introduced ***Suzie***, Bialosky's girlfriend. This antique reproduction was produced in several sizes and costumes, and its current value would be comparable to ***Bialosky*** prices.

A special thank you for their invaluable assistance in supplying information for this section goes to Bruce Raiffe and Shari Meltzer of Gund, Inc., and to long time friends Peggy and Alan Bialosky.

GEBRÜDER HERMANN KG

Hirschaid, Germany

The history of the **Gebrüder Hermann KG**, Teddy-Pluschspielwarenfabrik began in 1907 when Johann Hermann began the manufacture of teddy bears. He started his trade and business in a small workshop at Neufang near Sonneburg in Thuringia. His three sons and three daughters were all involved with the firm.

In 1903 Johann sent his oldest son, Bernhard, to Meiningen for an apprenticeship in trade and business to later join his brother already in the business. In 1911, Bernhard established his own business independent of his father and a year later married and moved to Sonneburg where he founded a small factory, employing several men and women in producing teddy bears and dolls. Sonneburg was recognized as the world's center for toy manufacturing, and several export houses were maintained here, including important American purchasers such as Woolworth, S.S. Kresge, George Borgfeldt, Louis Wolf and Sons, and others.

Bernhard Hermann and his wife had four sons, Hellmuth, Artur, Werner, and Horst. His oldest son, Hellmuth, was trained in the business and later established his own firm. Artur and Werner attended a commercial and industrial school, studying such things as designing, modelling and pattern making. After graduation they joined their father's firm.

In 1948 Bernhard Hermann and his three sons relocated the business and factory to Hirschaid near Bamberg, in the American zone of Germany. Since that time the firm has continued to prosper and grow, and Hermann has become one of the most famous manufacturers in the industry. In Sonneburg the business was named Bernhard Hermann, but in Hirschaid it was renamed the Teddy-Pluschspielwarenfabrik Gebrüder Hermann KG (Hermann Brothers Company, Manufacturers of Teddy Bears and Plush Toy Animals). The three sons became partners in the business.

Teddy bears have always been the number one product of this international firm. Many thousands of handmade teddy bears leave Hirshcaid every year and are shipped to destinations all over the world. Skilled employees, many of whom have been with the firm for decades, ensure the manufacture of well-designed and highly-finished toys. The Gebrüder Hermann KG continues the high ideals of the old firm in manufacturing only the finest quality handmade teddy bears and other soft toy animals for children and adult collectors alike.

The authors wish to extend a special thank you to Margit Drolshagen of Gebrüder Hermann KG, and to Peter and Anna Kalinke of Columbus, Ohio for their assistance in compiling the information for this section. Peter Kalinke is widely recognized as a leading authority on both well known and little known German teddy bear and doll producers. Mr. Kalinke lectures on the subject throughout the United States and frequently takes personally guided tours to Germany.

Anniversary Bear

This was the first limited edition produced by Gebrüder Hermann KG and was released in commemoration of their 75th Anniversary in 1986. It is a replica of a 1927 teddy. Fully jointed, made in tipped mohair. Growler. 16in (41cm) tall.

INTRODUCED: 1986

PRODUCTION: Limited Edition 3000

ORIGINAL PRICE: $150.00

CURRENT VALUE: $500.00

Tough Rudy
This is the first bear produced in distressed mohair by Gebrüder Hermann KG. 14in (36cm) tall, growler.
INTRODUCED: 1989
PRODUCTION: Limited Edition 2000
ORIGINAL PRICE: $120.00
CURRENT VALUE: $275.00

Young Bear
16in (41cm) bear, fully-jointed, growler. Produced in long tipped mohair. Discontinued 1986.
PRODUCTION: Open Edition
ORIGINAL PRICE: $100.00
CURRENT VALUE: $325.00

Angelica
14in (36cm) fully-jointed bear in white mohair with rose color paws. Wears a collar of white tulle with pink hearts. Pink bow in left ear.
INTRODUCED: 1988
PRODUCTION: Limited Edition 500
ORIGINAL PRICE: $110.00
CURRENT VALUE: $300.00

Music Bear
12in (31cm) full-jointed bear in cinnamon color mohair. Music box.
INTRODUCED: 1988
PRODUCTION: Limited Edition 500
ORIGINAL PRICE: $160.00
CURRENT VALUE: $450.00

Diane
12in (31cm) fully-jointed bear in pink color mohair. Wears pink lace collar.
INTRODUCED: 1988
PRODUCTION: Limited Edition 400
ORIGINAL PRICE: $100.00
CURRENT VALUE: $275.00

Bernhard Bear
22in (56cm) fully-jointed bear produced in long pile old gold mohair. Wears black and white striped vest with red bow tie.
INTRODUCED: 1988
PRODUCTION: Limited Edition 2000
ORIGINAL PRICE: $210.00
CURRENT VALUE: $525.00

Young Bear
14in (36cm) fully-jointed teddy in long tipped mohair. Growler.
INTRODUCED: 1989
PRODUCTION: Limited Edition 500
ORIGINAL PRICE: $110.00
CURRENT VALUE: $250.00

Epcot Bear
Limited edition 16in (41cm), fully-jointed bear made exclusively for **1989 Walt Disney World® Teddy Bear Convention**. Lemon color mohair, growler.
INTRODUCED: 1989
PRODUCTION: Limited Edition 500
ORIGINAL PRICE: $150.00
CURRENT VALUE: $375.00

Teddy Black
A 14in (36cm) fully-jointed bear in synthetic mink plush made exclusively for P. and E. Rubin, Inc. of Los Angeles, California. Also produced in 20in (51cm) size in white synthetic mink plush.
INTRODUCED: 1983
ORIGINAL PRICE: $120.00 (14in)
CURRENT VALUE: $650.00 (14in)

NORTH AMERICAN BEAR COMPANY

North American Bear Company has a very dedicated following that eagerly await the introduction of each of the distinctive bears in their V.I.B. (Very Important Bear) Collection. While this line continues to draw a strong response within the world of arctophiles, another line by this company quickly developed its own following. It was the introduction in 1983 of the Vanderbear family. The original family included the father ***Cornelius***, 20in (51cm) tall, mother ***Alice***, 18in (46cm) tall, brother ***Fuzzy***, 12in (31cm) tall and sister ***Fluffy***, 12in (31cm) tall. The following year a new addition to the family was welcomed. Her name is ***Muffy*** 7in (18cm) tall, and she has rapidly taken the bear collector world by storm.

One of the reasons for the strong appeal of ***Muffy*** is her wardrobe. She can be purchased with or without an original outfit, but the collector then has the option of adding to her wardrobe from a host of outfits. Muffy is equally loved by young and old alike, and has even developed her own fan club. Members are kept abreast of all news and developments related to ***Muffy***, and a special classified section allows members to buy and sell retired pieces. (See "Information Please" section.)

Muffy is offered to collectors as part of the Vanderbear collection, and also in a wide variety of designs by herself. Some of the designs have been retired, and some continue to be offered. Following is a partial listing of retired ***Muffy*** designs and their current secondary market values.

Muffy from the Limited Holiday Vanderbear Red Flannel Group.
INTRODUCED: 1985
ORIGINAL PRICE: $18.00
CURRENT VALUE: $475.00

Muffy Halloween Witch
Muffy wears witch's dress and hat and carries a mask.
INTRODUCED: 1986 (retired 1988)
ORIGINAL PRICE: $20.00
CURRENT VALUE: $600.00

The authors wish to offer a special Thank You to Penny Brode, company representative in Michigan, and to Susan A Leeson, Advertising and Public Relations Coordinator for North American Bear Company. Their assistance in providing information related to the company and the product line is greatly appreciated.

Muffy blue taffeta outfit from Vanderbear Taffeta Holiday collection.
INTRODUCED: 1986
ORIGINAL PRICE: $22.00
CURRENT VALUE: $475.00

Muffy Valentine I
Muffy wears a white eyelet dress with red heart necklace and hair bow.
INTRODUCED: 1986 (retired 1989)
ORIGINAL PRICE: $18.00
CURRENT VALUE: $400.00

Muffy in ballet outfit from Vanderbear Nutcracker Suite collection.
INTRODUCED: 1987
ORIGINAL PRICE: $23.50
CURRENT VALUE: $450.00

Muffy in skating outfit from Vanderbear Furrier and Ives collection.
INTRODUCED: 1988
ORIGINAL PRICE: $28.00
CURRENT VALUE: $325.00

Muffy Angel
Muffy wears a gold trimmed blue gown adorned with wings and a halo.
INTRODUCED: 1989
PRODUCTION: Limited Edition
ORIGINAL PRICE: $40.00
CURRENT VALUE: $100.00

Muffy Fir Tree
Muffy is costumed in green organdy and satin with a star and holly headdress, satin slippers and a partridge.
INTRODUCED: 1990
PRODUCTION: Limited Edition
ORIGINAL PRICE: $44.00
CURRENT VALUE: $125.00

Note: Secondary market prices for retired ***Muffy*** accessories are also very strong.

ROBERT RAIKES DESIGNS

This section contains listings of both Robert Raikes Originals (those produced entirely by the artist) and Robert Raikes bears designed by the artist and produced by Applause, Inc. Robert Raikes Originals qualify to be listed in the **Artist section**, but we felt it was important to list them together in the same section to avoid confusion.

Robert Raikes has been widely acclaimed as one of the finest artists in his medium of wood carving. He has captured the hearts of arctophiles the world over with his unique and heart warming wood face teddy bears. His first teddy bears were offered for sale in 1982, and today they are recreated and marketed around the world by Applause, Inc.

Robert did not receive the benefit of a formal art education or training. His drawing talents were inherited from his father, a cartoonist. His first carving was in junior high school, and he put it aside until 1969 when he served in the United States Navy and carved the word "love" on a block of wood and sent it to his teenage sweetheart, Carol (now his wife). After his tour of duty in the Navy, Bob enrolled in college where during a summer break, he met the noted wood carver Gilbert Valencia. Fascinated by Valencia's work, Bob spent his spare time observing and learning from the expert. By the end of the summer Bob purchased a set of tools and spent time developing his own style of carving.

Bob was determined to make carving his profession, and he worked 12 to 16 hours a day pursuing this goal. He first specialized in producing life-size birds and won awards for his work. A life-size pelican and many other examples of his work can be found today in Morro Bay, California.

In 1975 he created carved wooden dolls which were sold along with the other animals at craft shows and his parents' antique shop. With two children to raise, it was difficult for Bob and his wife to keep up with expenses. Since there seemed to be more demand for his dolls, he and Carol concentrated their efforts in this area. They produced 20 miniature dolls and offered them at their first doll show in 1981 where they were so well received by collectors that the Raikes made plans to do a major doll show. It took three months to produce 32 dolls for this show, and Bob's parents offered to do the show for them since they lived much closer. Before the show opened dealers were snapping up the dolls as fast as they were displayed. Robert Raikes, Sr., managed to set a few aside so they would have some to show the public. By noon on the first day of the show the dolls were completely sold out. Convinced that at last he had found his niche, Bob and Carol worked diligently to produce dolls for collectors.

Bob noticed the interest in teddy bears starting to surface at shows, so he added them to his work. Although they were not universally loved in the beginning, their popularity soon overtook that of his dolls. By 1984 it became apparent that the Raikes' could not hope to supply the demand for their work and a major manufacturer was sought to produce Bob's designs. A contract was signed with Applause, Inc. and history was made when the first edition of 7500 bears was sold out in three weeks. This unprecedented demand has continued unabated as each new edition is introduced.

Part of the success of Bob Raikes can certainly be attributed to his fascinating designs, but a large part can also be credited to his warm and sharing personality that is felt in each piece he creates. He is universally loved and respected by collectors and fellow artists wherever he goes.

A very detailed and excellently written story of Bob Raikes can be found in Linda Mullins recent book *The Raikes Bear and Doll Story* published by Hobby House Press, Inc. It is one of those rare books that one starts to read and simply cannot put down until you have reached the final page. This in-depth work gives you a complete look at Bob Raikes and his family, from their earliest struggles to make ends meet, to their well deserved international acclaim.

Information on the Robert Raikes Collectors Club can be found in the **Information Please section.**

The authors wish to express our gratitude to Bob Raikes, to Linda Mullins, and to Liz and Ed Oerding, "A Little Hug" for sharing their extensive knowledge and photographs for this section.

ROBERT RAIKES ORIGINAL BEARS
Designed and produced by the Artist
1982
One-of-a-kind teddy bear. An early Raikes original.
CURRENT VALUE:
$3800.00

1983
18in (46cm) ***Pouty bear*** by the Artist.
CURRENT VALUE:
$3700.00
18in (46cm) undressed bear by Bob Raikes.
CURRENT VALUE:
$3600.00

1984
12in (31cm) Raikes original bear (shown with Raikes' ***Little Red Riding Hood***). **CURRENT VALUE:** $2600.00 (bear only)
14in (36cm) Baby bears by Artist.
CURRENT VALUE:
$2600.00 each
24in (61cm) Raikes original wearing glasses and tie.
CURRENT VALUE:
$4200.00

1985
12in (31cm) ***Pilot bear*** by Bob Raikes.
CURRENT VALUE: $3400.00
24in (61cm) ***Ballet bear*** by Artist.
CURRENT VALUE: $4800.00
11in (28cm) all wood bear by Bob Raikes.
PRODUCTION: One-of-a-kind
CURRENT VALUE: $6000.00
24in (61cm) ***Country Boy*** and ***girl*** bears by Bob Raikes.
CURRENT VALUE: $4400.00 each

1987

Original 36in (91cm) ***Panda*** by the Artist.
PRODUCTION: One-of-a-kind
CURRENT VALUE: $4800.00
Artist's original ***Kevi*** (undressed) with painted eyes.
CURRENT VALUE: $2400.00
Ballerina in Spring. 18in (46cm) original.
CURRENT VALUE: $3200.00

1988
4½ foot high bear by the Artist.
PRODUCTION: One-of-a-kind
CURRENT VALUE: $6400.00

RAIKES BEARS BY APPLAUSE, INC.

Following is a list of teddy bears designed by Robert Raikes and produced by Applause, Inc. Values shown are approximate and reflect the secondary market prices in the fall of 1992. These are the best estimate of replacement values and are not intended to set prices. In some areas the prices may be higher or lower depending on supply and demand. Values are based on mint in box (MIB) condition with original box and certificate of authenticity. Any deviation from these conditions will devalue the price of the bears accordingly.

The bears in this section are from the private collection of Liz and Ed Oerding of Gleneden Beach, Oregon. The Oerdings started their collection of Raikes bears in the early part of 1986 and continued collecting until all individual pieces were in their collection. The Oerdings formed their business **A Little Hug** in January 1988 specializing in Raikes Bears exclusively. Their extensive experience specializing in retired Raikes Bears by Applause has given the Oerdings an excellent knowledge of Raikes bear values. Raikes collectors may contact the Oerdings at the address shown in **Important Addresses section.**

We wish to thank the Oerdings for sharing their knowledge and their collection with us. *Photographs by Larry Kirkwood.*

NOTE: All bears listed are fully jointed, with wooden face and feet, and made in synthetic plush, unless otherwise stated.

1985
SEBASTIAN
First Edition. 21in (53cm) tall. Wears brown plaid vest, bow tie, brass spectacles.
PRODUCTION: Limited Edition 7500
ORIGINAL PRICE: $100.00
CURRENT VALUE: $375.00

REBECCA
First Edition. 21in (53cm) tall. Wears bright red dress with off-white pinafore and red satin bow on her head.
PRODUCTION: Limited Edition 7500
ORIGINAL PRICE: $100.00
CURRENT VALUE: $850.00

ERIC
First Edition. 15in (38cm) tall. Wears bright blue knitted ski sweater, hat and scarf. ***Eric*** is the first "pout mouth" Raikes bear by Applause.
PRODUCTION: Limited Edition 7500
ORIGINAL PRICE: $65.00
CURRENT VALUE: $650.00

CHELSEA
First Edition. 15in (38cm) tall. Wears off white dress with blue and rust flower pattern.
PRODUCTION: Limited Edition 7500
ORIGINAL PRICE: $65.00
CURRENT VALUE: $1200.00

1986

TYRONE

Second Edition. 36in (91cm) tall. Jointed arms and legs only. Wooden face, feet, paw pads and eye lashes. Wears black tuxedo and vest, white shirt and tie. Largest Raikes bear released by Applause.
PRODUCTION: Limited Edition 5000
ORIGINAL PRICE: $300.00
CURRENT VALUE: $950.00

CHRISTOPHER

Second Edition. 15in (38cm) tall. "Pout mouth." Dressed in sailor suit.
PRODUCTION: Limited Edition 15000
ORIGINAL PRICE: $65.00
CURRENT VALUE: $475.00

PENELOPE
Second Edition. 15in (38cm) tall. Wears pink satin dress trimmed in lace.
PRODUCTION: Limited Edition 15000
ORIGINAL PRICE: $65.00
CURRENT VALUE: $675.00

MAX
Second Edition. 21in (53cm) tall. Dressed in card dealer outfit complete with visor and arm band.
PRODUCTION: Limited Edition 15000
ORIGINAL PRICE: $100.00
CURRENT VALUE: $300.00

BRIDE AND GROOM
Special Edition. Each 15in (38cm) tall. Set came in large box and each numbered on foot.
PRODUCTION: Limited Edition 15000 (only 10000 produced)
ORIGINAL PRICE: $150.00 set
CURRENT VALUE: $675.00 set

ZELDA
Third Edition. 15in (38cm) tall. "Pout mouth." Wears black fringed "flapper" dress, black sequined head band, pink pearl necklace and black garter. A very popular Raikes bear.
PRODUCTION: Limited Edition 15000
ORIGINAL PRICE: $65.00
CURRENT VALUE: $600.00

LINDY
Third Edition. 21in (53cm) tall. Wears flight jacket, cap with goggles, and flying ace scarf. One of the most sought after Raikes bears.
PRODUCTION: Limited Edition 15000
ORIGINAL PRICE: $100.00
CURRENT VALUE: $925.00

1987
CALVIN AND REBECCA
First Edition Rabbits. Each 18in (46cm) tall. Heads and ears carved from wood, wooden pin-jointed hands and feet. A quality problem limited production to approximately 1200 sets, making these rabbits highly sought after.
PRODUCTION: Limited Edition 5000 (actual production 1200 sets)
ORIGINAL PRICE: $150.00 set
CURRENT VALUE: $1100.00 set

CASEY
Fourth Edition. 15in (38cm) tall. Wearing red, white and blue baseball uniform, left handed mitt. Number 37 printed on back of jersey.
PRODUCTION: Limited Edition 7500
ORIGINAL PRICE: $65.00
CURRENT VALUE: $275.00

1988

SALLY
Fifth Edition. 15in (38cm) tall. Wears pink flowered cotton dress.
PRODUCTION: Limited Edition 7500
ORIGINAL PRICE: $75.00
CURRENT VALUE: $225.00

ANNIE
First Mother's Day bear. 15in (38cm) tall. Wooden face is heart shaped. Wears pink and white cotton dress with pink satin bow on head.
PRODUCTION: Limited Edition 7500
ORIGINAL PRICE: $80.00
CURRENT VALUE: $300.00

SANTA AND MRS. CLAUS
First Christmas Edition. Each are 18in (46cm) tall. Both bears costumed in deep wine color velveteen. ***Santa's*** beard, eyebrows and moustache are carved wood and painted white. ***Mrs Claus*** wears brass wire spectacles.
PRODUCTION: Limited Edition 7500 each
ORIGINAL PRICE: $100.00 each
CURRENT VALUE: $275.00 each

1989

LIONEL
Seventh Edition. 16in (41cm) tall. Dressed in striped blue engineer overalls with matching cap and traditional red bandana on neck.
PRODUCTION: Limited Edition 10000
ORIGINAL PRICE: $75.00
CURRENT VALUE: $225.00

SANTA CLAUS
Second Edition Santa. 16in (41cm) tall. Moustache, beard and eyebrows carved from wood and painted white. Dressed in traditional red Santa outfit with large wooden belt buckle.
PRODUCTION: Limited Edition 7500
ORIGINAL PRICE: $100.00
CURRENT VALUE: $300.00

BILLY BUCCANEER AND M'LADY HONEYPOT
First Robert Raikes Collector Club Convention Edition. Each are 12in (31cm) tall. Both bears numbered on foot, certificate and special box. ***Billy Buccaneer*** wears a classy pirate outfit with eye patch. Wood peg leg. ***M'Lady Honeypot*** wears a coordinated outfit to compliment the pair.
PRODUCTION: Limited Edition 2500 sets
ORIGINAL PRICE: $195.00 set
CURRENT VALUE: $550.00 set

1990
COURT JESTER
Ninth Edition. 16in (41cm) tall. Wears elegant court jester outfit and holds a wooden faced Jester head on a stick with a matching outfit.
PRODUCTION: Limited Edition 10000
ORIGINAL PRICE: $110.00
CURRENT VALUE: $275.00

NOTE: This is not a complete listing of Raikes bears by Applause, due to space limitations.

Margarete Steiff GmbH
Giengen (Brenz)
Germany

For over one hundred years the **Margarete Steiff Co.**, has been producing unique and innovative toys. Based on the philosophy of their founder, Margarete, "Only the best is good enough..." this company manufactures new and reproduction pieces to the highest standards of old world craftsmanship.

The company was founded in 1880 in Giengen, Germany by Margarete Steiff. The first piece she created was a small elephant pincushion. This led the way to a whole menagerie of different species and sizes of animals including dolls. Their early products were primarily made of fine felt. In 1902 Richard Steiff, Margarete's nephew, designed a fully-jointed bear made of mohair plush. The mohair made the bear look very realistic. The joints allowed it to be posed in many positions giving it an individuality. Later this style bear became known as the teddy bear and has provided enjoyment to generations of children and adults.

Because of the great values put on original antique pieces, Steiff's reproduction pieces have been highly sought after by collectors. These reproduction pieces are manufactured as closely as possible to the originals. Since they are produced in small world wide quantities a supply and demand situation exists which has caused many of the reproduction pieces to escalate in value.

Steiff antique teddy bears have consistently brought the highest prices at auctions throughout the world, and we have every confidence that this same leadership role will continue as some of their more current pieces reach the secondary market.

Steiff Original Teddy #0153/43
Replica of 1905 original, produced in 1980 for Steiff's 100th Anniversary. 17in (43cm) in mohair fabric, stuffed with wood shavings. Came in a presentation box with certificate (6000 English, 5000 German).
INTRODUCED: 1980
PRODUCTION: Limited Edition 11000 worldwide
ORIGINAL PRICE: $150.00
CURRENT VALUE: $1100.00

Steiff Original Teddy Bear Set #0155/38
Widely recognized as the ***Mother and Baby bear set*** to compliment the ***Papa Original Teddy*** produced the previous year. Reproductions of 1905 originals. ***Mother bear*** 15in (38cm), ***Baby*** is 6¼in (16cm) tall. Mohair fabric, white ear tag. Special gift box with signed certificate.
INTRODUCED: 1981
PRODUCTION: Limited Edition 8000 United States Market only
ORIGINAL PRICE: $150.00 set
CURRENT VALUE: $950.00 set

Tea Party Set #0204/16
Set consisted of four 6¼in (16cm) bears in various colors, accompanied by a china tea service made in Germany. 1905 reproductions. Mohair fabric. Special gift box resembled a room with dishes on a table in center. Bears identified with white ear tags. Certificate.
INTRODUCED: 1982
PRODUCTION: Limited Edition 10000 sets
ORIGINAL PRICE: $170.00 set
CURRENT VALUE: $650.00 set

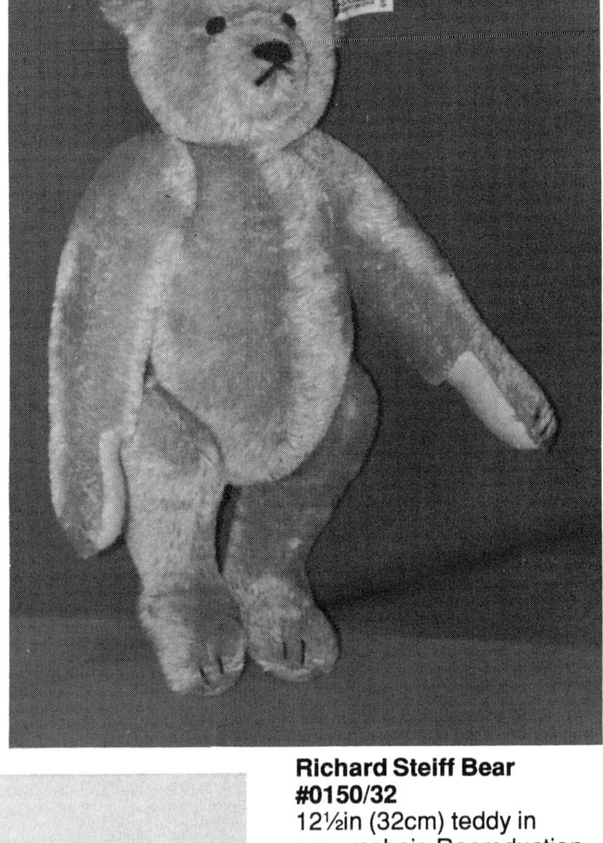

Richard Steiff Bear #0150/32
12½in (32cm) teddy in gray mohair. Reproduction of 1905 original which was designed by Richard Steiff. Steiff's first bear to use the disc and pin joint system. Gift box. White ear tag.
INTRODUCED: 1983
PRODUCTION: Approximately 20000 pieces
ORIGINAL PRICE: $100.00
CURRENT VALUE: $475.00

Margaret Strong Chocolate Teddy Bear Set #0160/00
Set included 4 bears in sizes 7in (18cm), 10in (25cm), 12in (31cm),and 16½in (42cm). Produced in chocolate color mohair. Leather pads. White ear tags.
INTRODUCED: 1983
PRODUCTION: Limited Edition 11000 pieces
ORIGINAL PRICE: $275.00 set
CURRENT VALUE: $950.00 set

Gold Teddy 1909 #0165/28
Reproduction of a 1909 original. Gold mohair. Yellow ear tag. 11in (28cm) tall.
INTRODUCED: 1984
ORIGINAL PRICE: $62.00
CURRENT VALUE: $175.00

Panda Bear #0178/35
1938 replica, 14in (36cm) in mohair. Yellow ear tag, folded double cloth. Same model produced in 1992 with single cloth ear tag.
INTRODUCED: 1984
ORIGINAL PRICE: $110.00
CURRENT VALUE: $425.00

Mr. Cinnamon Bear #0151/32
12½in (32cm) teddy in mohair. Yellow ear tag. Replica of 1903 bears. Name taken from book by Sara Tawney Lefferts that contained illustrations of this bear.
INTRODUCED: 1984
ORIGINAL PRICE: $90.00
CURRENT VALUE: $500.00

Dicky Bear #0172/32
13½in (34cm) mohair bear. Pads and mouth with special paint treatment. Reproduction of 1930 original. White ear tag. Gift box certificate.
INTRODUCED: 1985
PRODUCTION: Limited Edition 20000 world wide
ORIGINAL PRICE: $99.50
CURRENT VALUE: $250.00

Teddy Clown Bear #0170/32
Replica of 1926 original. White ear tag. 12½in (32cm) high. Wears felt hat and neck ruff.
INTRODUCED: 1986
PRODUCTION: Limited Edition 10000 pieces
ORIGINAL PRICE: $150.00
CURRENT VALUE: $400.00

Teddy Clown Driver #0163/19
7½in (19cm) pre-1910 replica. Produced as driver for the Circus Train Calliope Wagon. Wears clown hat and blouse.
INTRODUCED: 1987
PRODUCTION: Limited Edition 5000 pieces
ORIGINAL PRICE: $58.00
CURRENT VALUE: $275.00

Gieng-Ling Panda #0218/14
A limited edition panda produced exclusively for Festival of Steiff sponsored by The Toy Store (formerly Hobby Center Toys) in Toledo, Ohio. 5½in (14cm) tall with white ear tag. Mohair fabric.
INTRODUCED: 1988
PRODUCTION: Limited Edition 1000 pieces
ORIGINAL PRICE: $60.00
CURRENT VALUE: $275.00

UK Bear #0174/61
1907 replica produced for the British market. 23½in (60cm) tall in mohair. White ear tag.
INTRODUCED: 1989
PRODUCTION: Limited Edition 2000 pieces
ORIGINAL PRICE: $300.00
CURRENT VALUE: $950.00

Polar Bear #0090/11
4in (10cm) bear with jointed legs and special ball jointed neck. Replica of 1909 original in Steiff Museum collection. Gift box.
INTRODUCED: 1987
PRODUCTION: Limited Edition 3000 pieces
ORIGINAL PRICE: $95.00
CURRENT VALUE: $300.00

SECTION THREE

INFORMATION PLEASE

This section contains a listing of contacts and addresses for a number of Teddy Bear Clubs devoted to various collector bears, manufacturers' addresses, and the address for Good Bears of the World.

COLLECTOR TEDDY BEAR CLUBS

Canterbury Bear Collectors Society
P.O. Box 47
Valparaiso, Indiana 46384
Donna L. Saqui, President
Newsletter is sent to members with news of new developments in Canterbury Bears, appearances by the Blackburns, exchange of ideas and latest developments pertaining to Canterbury Bears.

Muffy Vanderbear Club
North American Bear Company, Inc.
401 N. Wabash, Suite 500
Chicago, Illinois 60611
This club was formed by the North American Bear Company to keep Muffy's many collectors informed of new developments, through a newsletter published three times a year. It also keeps members informed of Muffy appearances around the country, and offers the opportunity to purchase a Limited Edition Muffy for members only.

Robert Raikes Collectors Club
P.O. Box 82
Mount Shasta, California 96067
A one time lifetime membership fee includes a Limited Edition Raikes Bear for members only, annual convention, quarterly newsletter provides up-to-date information on Raikes activities, new releases, etc. A complete story about the Robert Raikes Collectors Club can be found in Linda Mullins' book *The Raikes Bear & Doll Story* published by Hobby House Press, Inc.

GOOD BEARS OF THE WORLD

This nonprofit organization publishes a quarterly magazine called *Bear Tracks* that keeps members posted on stories of their primary function, which is to supply teddy bears to children in hospitals, to police, and paramedic agencies for use with traumatized children, and to senior citizens in need of a companion. They have dens (clubs) throughout the world, and individual members. Current copy of magazine and complete membership information available for $1.00.
Good Bears of the World
P.O. Box 13097
Toledo, Ohio 43613

MANUFACTURERS OF COLLECTOR TEDDY BEARS

- Applause, Inc. (Robert Raikes Collector Bears)
  6101 Variel Ave.
  P.O. Box 4183
  Woodland Hills, California 91365-4183
- Robert Raikes' Specialist
  Liz and Ed Oerding
  P.O. Box 317
  Gleneden Beach, Oregon 97388
- Bearly There, Inc.
  14782 Moran St.
  Westminster, California 92683
- Blessed Companion Bear Company
  507 Ash St.
  Lake Oswego, Oregon 97034
- Gund, Inc.
  P.O. Box H
  Edison, New Jersey 08818
- Gebrüder Hermann KG
  Postfach 1207
  D8606 Hirschaid
  GERMANY

Additional information on Hermann and other German companies:

- Peter Kalinke
  641 S. Spring Rd.
  Westerville, Ohio 43081
- Steiff USA LP
  200 Fifth Ave., Suite 1205
  New York, New York 10010

Note: Artist addresses are shown with each artist listing.

ARTIST INDEX

Adams, Joanne: 7
Alberstadt, Barbara: 8
Allen, Darlene: 8
Allen, Durae: 9
Altherr, Terri L.: 10

Babb, Diane: 11
Baker, Susan: 12
Baldo, Mary Fran: 13
Baloun, Sherry: 13
Beck, Doris: 14
Bedwell, Debra: 15-16
Black, Carol: 15
Blair, Patricia: 16
Bonner, Jan: 17-18
Brame, Ginger: 19
Brittsan, Deanna: 20
Bronzino, Barbara and Brown, JoAnn: 20-21
Brown, Barbara: 21
Buttitta, Genie: 22

Calvin, Karen and Howard: 23-24
Cavallero, Carol: 24
Chang, Rosalind: 25
Claustre, Donna: 25
Crowe, Nancy: 26
Cubillas, Corla: 27

Dahle, Elizabeth: 27-28
DePee, Suzanne: 28
Dewire, Denise: 29
Dickl, Sandra: 29
Diddier, Deborah: 29
Duvall, Deanna: 29-30
Dyer, Holly: 31

Egbert, Paula: 32
Egelin, Tatum: 32-33

Fici, Patricia: 33-34
Fleming, Sandy: 34-35
Foskey, Sue and Randall: 36-37
Franks, Gloria: 37
Freeman, Chester: 38
Frischmann, Rosalie: 38

Gadano, Jean and Fry, Mitzi: 39
Gamble, Elaine Fujita: 40
Gard, Diane: 40-41
Gatto, Lynn: 42
Gill, Patricia: 42
Green, Jeanne: 43-44

Haggard, Mary: 44
Hahn, Lillian: 45
Harrell, Serieta: 45
Harrison, Dickie: 46-47
Haught, Rhonda: 47
Hayes, Terry: 48
Henderson, Billee: 49
Henry, Mike and Linda: 49-51
Hilgendorf, Betsy: 51
Hines, Deborah and Derik: 52
Hockenberry, Dee: 52
Hodges, Donna: 53
Howey, Shirley: 54-55
Hughes, Elva: 55-56

Inman, Ann: 56

Katzopoulos, Linda: 57
King, Barbara: 57
King, Doris: 58
Koch, Barbara J.: 58
Krantz, Jenny: 59
Kynion, Ann: 60

Landstra, Bev Miller: 61
LaPointe, Sharon: 61
Laverty, Lois: 62
Lecrone, Mary Kay: 63
Leistikow, Althea: 64
Lockwood, Wendy: 64
Low, Donna: 65

McClellan, Sarah: 65
McConnell, Barbara: 66
McElwain, Maureen Covert: 66-67
Malcolm, Melodie: 67
Mannon, Becky: 68
Martin, Carol and Henry: 68-69
Martin, Carolyn B.: 70
Martin, Cindy: 70-71
Masor, Sher: 72
Masterson, Karine: 72
Mead, Linda: 73
Mediate, Flora: 73
Michaud, Doris and Terry: 74
Milton, Zelma: 75
Mitchell, Joanne: 75-76
Morris, Jackie: 76
Murphy, Pat: 76

Nagle, Susan Webber: 77
Nearing, Kathy: 77
Neaves, Mary: 77
Nett, Gary and Margaret: 78
Newlin, Sue: 79
Nicholl, Dawn: 79

Orlando, Cat: 80
O'Sullivan, Joyce: 80

Pauk, Christina Hemmet: 81-82
Pearce, Carol: 83
Phillippi, Neysa: 83-84
Phillips, Gary Lee: 84
Phillips, Sara: 85-86
Policky, Rose: 86

Quinn, Sue: 87

Raikes, Robert: 136-150
Rankin, Jodi: 88
Reeves, Janet: 88-89
Rixon, Susan: 89

Schmidt, Maria: 90
Schutt, Steve: 91-92
Seiple, Edda: 92
Shaw, Denis: 93
Shum, Linda Suzanne: 93-94
Sours, Monty and Joe: 94
Stewart, Carol: 95
Suarez, Betty: 95
Swanson, Judith: 96

Tipton, Colleen: 96
Tomlinson, Patricia: 97
Troxel, Barbara A.: 97
Turner, Laura: 97

Veins, Margaret: 98

Wallace, Kathleen: 98-99
Warlow, Gerry: 100
Waugh, Carol-Lynn Rössell: 100
Whisnant, Barbara: 101
White, Bev: 101
Woessner, Joan: 102-103
Wooley, Pamela: 104
Wright, Beverly Martin: 105
Wright, Nan: 105-106

Zimmerman, Marie: 106

TRADE NAME INDEX

Annemade — Ann Inman, 56

B & J Originals — Barbara Bronzino and JoAnn Brown: 20-21
B.J.'s Bears & My Honey's Woods — Barbara J. Koch: 58
Ballard Baines Bears — Karen and Howard Calvin: 23-24
Barbara King Bears — Barbara King: 57
Barbara's Bears — Barbara Brown: 21
Barbear & Friends, Ltd. — Barbara Whisnant: 101
Barrington Bears — ELva Hughes: 55-56
Beana Bears, Etc. — Ann Kynion: 60
Bear Den Hollow — Barbara A. Troxel: 97
Bear Elegance — Joan Woessner: 102-103
Bearhearts — Carol Black: 15-16
Bear House, The — Lillian Hahn: 45
Bearish Delights — Denise DeWire: 29
Bear Lady, The — Monty and Joe Sours: 94
Bearloom Bears — Mike and Linda Henry: 49-51
Bearons of La Jolla, The — Donna Hodges: 53
Bears, Bears & Bears — Betty Suarez: 95
Bears by Althea — Althea Leistikow: 64
Bears by Jodi — Jodi Rankin: 88
Bears by Nett — Gary and Margaret Nett: 78
Bear Works — Christina Hemmett Pauk: 81-82
Bev Landstra Collectables — Bev Miller Landstra: 61
Blacklick Bears — Jackie Morris: 76
Blair Bears — Patricia Blair: 16
Bonner Bears & Friends — Jan Bonner: 17-18
Buttonbush — Jeanne Green: 43-44

cm Bears — Carol and Henry Martin: 68-69
Carrousel by Michaud — Doris and Terry Michaud: 74
Catskill Honey Bears — Barbara Alberstadt: 8
Charlestowne Bear, The — Maria Schmidt: 90
Collee Bears — Colleen Tipton: 96
Country & Bears — Wendy Lockwood: 64
Custom Teddy Bears — Carol Stewart: 95

Dancing Needle, The — Corla Cubillis: 27
D'Bears — Debra Bedwell: 15
Debearahs — Deborah Diddier: 29
Denis's Den — Denis Shaw: 93
Diane Gard Enterprises — Diane Gard40-41
Donna Claustre Originals — Donna Claustre: 25
Dori's Bears — Doris Beck: 14
Doris King Originals — Doris King: 58
Dormouse Designs — Sue Quinn: 87

Family Tree Bears — Joanne Mitchell: 75-76
Fancy Stuffins — Melodie Malcolm: 67
Flora's Teddys — Flora Mediate: 73
Fujita-Gamble Teddies — Elaine Fujita Gamble: 40
Fur Real Bears — Judith Swanson: 96

Genie B's Bears — Genie Buttitta: 22
Gerry's Teddy & Craft Designs — Gerry Warlow: 100
Gile Teddy Bears — Lois Laverty: 62
Goose Creek — Gloria Franks: 37-38
Grae Waki Bears — Dawn Nicholl: 79

Haggard Huggables — Mary Haggard: 44
Handmade Bears by Deanna Brittsan — Deanna Brittsan: 20-21
Happy Tymes Collectables — Bev White: 101
Hollybearys — Holly Dyer: 31
Honeypot Bears — Suzanne De Pee: 28
Hug-A-Bear — Janet Reeves: 88-89

J.D. Babb, Inc — Diane Babb: 11

Karine's — Karine Masterson: 72

LeBear's — Mary Kay Lecrone: 63
Lil' Honeys by Durae — Durae Allen: 9
Limerick Bear, Inc. — Lynn Gatto: 42
Linda's Bear-iety Bears — Linda Katzopoulos: 57
Liz's Tender Loving Teddies — Elizabeth Dahle: 27-28

McB Bears — Barbara McConnell: 66
M.F.B. Enterprises — Mary Fran Baldo: 13
Mama Bear Creations — Mary Neaves: 77
Marsh Creek Bears — Maureen Covert McElwain: 66-67
Maul & Paw — Rhonda Haught: 47
Mill Creek Creations — Rosalie Frischmann: 38
My Bears & Whimsy — Deanna Duvall: 29-30
My Kind of Bear — Kathy Nearing: 77
Murphy Bears — Pat Murphy: 76

Need Just A Bear — Joyce O'Sullivan: 80
Nonsuch Soft Toys — Rixon, Susan, 89
Nostalgic Bear Co. — Sue and Randall Foskey: 36-37

Ohio River Bear Co. — Susan Baker: 12
Olde Tyme Toys & Treasures — Nan Wright: 105-106
Original Bitte Schoen Bears — Sherry Baloun: 13
Owassa Bear Co. — Jenny Krantz: 59
Oz-Born Collectibles — Patricia Tomlinson: 97

Panda Monium — Terri L. Altherr: 10
Pandas Plus — Donna Low: 65
Paw Quette — Marie Zimmerman: 106
Pearls — Nancy Crowe: 26
Pendleton's Teddy Bears — Terry Hayes: 48
Piece Parade, The — Ginger Brame: 19-20
Purely Neysa — Neysa Phillippi: 83-84
Purple Crayon Creations — Betsy Hilgendorf: 51

Rak-a-Ree-Bos — Margaret Veins: 98
Raspbeary Bears — Darlene Allen: 8
River Hills Bears — Edda Seiple: 92
Rosebearys — Carol Pearce: 83
Roz Bears — Rosalind Chang: 25

Sal's Pals — Sarah McClellan: 65
Sandy Fleming Bears — Sandy Fleming: 34-35
Sankar Bears & Buddies — Sandra Dickl: 29
Sersha Collectibles — Serieta Harrell: 45
Shirley Howey Bears — Shirley Howey: 54-55
Stier Bears — Kathleen Wallace: 98-99
Storybook Bears — Joanne Adams: 7
Sue Newlin Collectibles — Sue Newlin: 79

Susie's Sewn Originals — Susan Webber Nagle: 77

Tabby's Bears — Jean Gadano and Mitzi Fry: 39
Taddy Bears — Carol Cavallero: 24
Tea-Bere-Y Hollow Originals — Linda Mead: 73
Ted E. Tail Originals — Linda Suzanne Shum: 93-94
Teddy Bear Blessings — Deborah and Derik Hines: 52
Teddy Bear Heaven — Paula Egbert: 32
Trishka's Treasures — Patricia Fici: 33-34

Wicker Buggy, The — Sher Masor: 72
Windsor Cottage Crafts — Laura Turner: 97
Woodhaven Cottage — Patricia Gill: 42
Wooley Bear Cottage — Pamela Wooley: 104
Wright Bear, The — Beverly Martin Wright: 105

Yesterbears — Cindy Martin: 70-71

Z & J Enterprises — Zelma Milton: 75

MANUFACTURER INDEX

Bearly There, Inc.: 108-114
Blessed Companion Bear Company: 115-117

Canterbury Bears, Ltd.: 118-123

Gund, Inc.: 124-128
Gerbrüder Hermann KG: 129-132

North American Bear Company, Inc.: 133-135

Robert Raikes Designs (Originals & Applause, Inc.): 136-150

Margarete Steiff GmbH: 151-155

ABOUT THE AUTHORS

Doris and Terry Michaud are internationally recognized for their expertise in the teddy bear world. They have been designing and producing handcrafted teddies since the late 1970s. They have an extensive collection of antique teddy bears, and travel extensively throughout the world giving lectures on the subject, and conducting teddy bear making seminars.

The Michauds also write articles and columns for a number of teddy bear and collector magazines here and abroad. They have written three books, all published by Hobby House Press, Inc.: *Bears Repeating, Stories Old Teddy Bears Tell*; *How To Make & Sell Quality Teddy Bears*; *Teddy Tales, Bears Repeating Too.*

The Michauds' award-winning teddies are marketed under the trade name Carrousel by Michaud and are sold throughout the United States and in four other countries. They own and operate Carrousel, a charming collector's shop located in an 1895 Victorian home in Chesaning, Michigan, where they also display their unique teddy bear collection.